Stolen Options

AN AUTOBIOGRAPHY
BY
MAE EDWARDS

To Dwayne & Louise

Mae Edwards

PUBLISHED BY ONNEY PUBLISHING & PERFORMANCES, INC

Dedication

I'd like to thank my daughter, husband, and especially my friend Mattie, who encouraged me throughout this process and stood by me in the hard times, also my friends Lorretta and Sherrie, for being there when I really needed a friend. Don't let stereotypes keep you down. If you think you can do something, don't let others keep you from it. Where there's a will there's a Mae.

About the Author

Mae Edwards, was born Mabelle Juanita Hague in Wichita, Kansas. She is number six of seven children, who were separated when she was three. Mae grew up in Houston, Texas, while in foster care through the DePelchin Faith Home (now the DePelchin Children's Center).

"Stolen Options" is the story of how she survived the constant moving around from home to home, the Air Force, an abusive husband, and beyond. Upon surviving some of the toughest years in an unhealthy marriage, Mae later got remarried, this time to her high school sweetheart. She is now a part of a very loving and successful marriage. She currently resides in Waller, Texas, and enjoys riding her motorcycle with her husband, hiking in the mountains, target shooting, traveling, photography, making jewelry, and ceramics. She also enjoys collecting Barbie's, antique souvenir spoons, coins, stamps, and old cameras.

Mae is the proud business owner of Personalize Photo, (her first love of the arts), Trimsandmore, (specializing in products that will help improve septic systems in municipalities and personal systems), and Mary Kay. Being a veteran herself, she stands in support of the Wounded Warrior's non-profit organization.

She has two children, and two biological grandchildren; but by marriage have an additional five grandchildren and five great-grand-children. She strongly believes that all things are possible through God and Faith; as she knows that He has a plan for us all. Despite all that she has been through, she feels that writing has been a way of healing her soul. Mae decided to share her story, in hopes to help others see that horrible deeds done to oneself by others, does not have to determine your future or the path you decide to take in life.

Preface

'America the Beautiful', do you really mean it when you say it? Do we really appreciate what we see of America? Just what do you see? Are you heading down to Cozumel, Mexico, or off to Italy on your vacations?

I've jetted to New York City, Seattle, Atlanta, Las Vegas and Los Angeles. I've been to Guam, Wyoming, and Florida. I have seen the cities un-scrubbed and washed, but I have also seen the amber glow of sunsets, snowcapped mountaintops and the changing colors of the oceans. This country that our ancestors fought for in wars, boardrooms and in Congress is out there for all of us to enjoy and share with our children and grandchildren. Have you been to a park lately? Biked around town or been on a car trip with your family?

What do you look at when you are on a plane? I always try to get a window seat because I like to see what I am going to be around. I try to see landmarks and get a general direction of where things are, like bodies of water, mountains, towers, etc.

When we are riding our motorcycles around the mountain curves, I think, my God! what a beautiful painting you've made. To experience the deep blue water around Guam with the coral reef is an unspeakable wonder. We have such a splendid country. I'm not saying that the rest of the world isn't beautiful, but we take pride in our country and want to enjoy everything that it has to offer before the laws prevent us from doing what we love so much. Some countries don't allow the freedom to travel as we do in the U.S.

I try to take advantage of every place I visit, after all, God put it here for us to enjoy. I've lived my life to the fullest and taken every chance to do what others said was not proper for a girl to do. You can try and tell me, "you can't do this or that," but I won't listen. I really don't take "no" for an answer. When I was a young girl, everyone seemed to take my options away from me. I was told where to live and with whom. I was determined, as an adult, that I would take advantage of all options available to me.

These are the stories of my upbringing. Some have been confirmed or told to me by my siblings and foster parents. Most of the names have been changed to protect the privacy of my friends and loved ones.

There were many people in my life that helped to guide me and shape the person I am today. Bad things happen to everyone. How you handle it, and what you take from that experience, is up to you.

Table of Contents

The Beginning

When I was young, I can remember that I felt so alone, but for one silent friend that seemed to always keep me company in my times of trouble, which seemed to be all the time. Most kids have invisible friends. Mine just happened to be Jesus. Though I didn't really have a full understanding of the spirituality aspect, I just knew. I was told that God never gives us more than we can handle, and he puts people in our paths that will be there to guide us through life. I guess it just hit a cord within my soul that made me realize that Jesus was always there watching over me.

Some people say that a person can only remember as far back as the earliest, most traumatic event in their life. I can remember when we lived in Kansas and I was crying in my crib. I can see the bunk-beds where my siblings slept in our room. I couldn't have been more than one-year old. I can also remember being around two and trying to get my sister Annette out of my rocker; we were wearing Easter hats. When talking with my siblings later in life, I discussed this with them and found the memories to be true.

I have only one item from my childhood, a doll named Suzi. She is red haired, cloth bodied, with rubber limbs and head. When my mother gave her to me, as an adult, she didn't have much hair. She said that I used to carry her around by the hair, so there was only a small wisp of red hair at the top of her head. I eventually had her body remade and a wig. I was told that I carried her everywhere with me. My grandmother had given her to me on my second birthday.

There are several stories that my siblings tell me of our life while in Wichita. One time, the older kids decided to build a shack with mud bricks. They made the walls first, and just as the roof was being applied, the neighbor came and made them tear it down because it was on government land. Later, my dad decided to build a garage onto the house. He started with the roof since

1

the neighbor had complained before, and after a wall was built, here goes the neighbor again, making him tear it down because it was not supposed to be attached to the house. The reasons...I am not clear on. Dad dug out an earthen basement or crawl space under the house. I do remember something about some dirt tunnels. I was told that this was where we would shelter if a tornado warning was in effect.

I am number six from a family of seven children. I was named after my two grandmothers, Mabel and Bell, as a result, Mabelle. I've hated the name my entire life. On the Beverly Hillbillies, Elly Mae had a monkey named Mabelle, Gomer Pyle had a cow named Mabelle, and then later on I found a dog named Mabelle. I just couldn't win. The only saving grace was that the phone operator's name on the Dukes of Hazard was also Mabelle; she was cute.

We were a family of two boys and five girls. With two adults and seven children, we ate at a picnic table. We lived in a two-bedroom house, and my mother would bake a lot and sew for us a little bit. I guess with so many kids, who had time to sew? I remember one story about when the flour and sugar would go on sale. My mother would buy a fifty-pound sack of each, then Dad's parents would come for a visit and purchase another sack of each. Mother said that she baked for quite a while.

The four oldest were born in Houston, TX, and the three youngest in Wichita, KA. My fraternal grandparents lived in Illinois and my maternal grandparents lived in Houston, TX. In 1962, my maternal grandfather died of skin melanoma. When my mother divorced my father, my grandmother, Munnie, convinced her to come to Houston and live with her.

My grandfather had been a postmaster in Boston, then he went to work with the Union Pacific Railroad, and later, the Gulf Oil Company. Munnie, my grandmother, took care of the family and encouraged my mother to go to college, thinking that she would meet someone and get married. Mother went to the University of Illinois, where she met my father. She did finish her degree, majoring in music.

I later found out that Munnie was as manipulative as my father, but maybe that was the only way they knew how to be. She had convinced Mother to come down to stay with her to help her get away from my dad. I believe she just wanted a companion. After we were there for a little while, she decided that we were too much for her. Mother was taking parenting classes through The Children's Home; we just called it "The Home". I guess she was just overwhelmed with seven kids and needed to understand how to manage such a large family.

We eventually moved into an apartment in Houston, and my mother started counseling with "The Home". She also started taking classes to get certified to become a music teacher. She had majored in music in college and needed her teacher's certification to teach in the school system. While she was in classes, the older kids took care of the younger ones. They were very responsible kids, but Munnie finally paid someone to come and stay with us while Mother was in classes.

While living with Munnie, Betsy broke both her arms, while climbing from tree to tree, in the front yard. At the same time, I was walking across the street. I was about two years old, I believe. Betsy fell out of the tree, ran and grabbed me, and carried me back to the house, not knowing that she had broken both her arms.

Mother was not a very stable person, emotionally. With her husband and mother, both controlling her, it was no wonder that she wound up in the state hospital with a nervous breakdown. During this time, Munnie placed us with various church families for a temporary solution. She certainly couldn't handle all of us. I think she really wanted a companion and found out that mother was just too unstable.

My dad came down from Kansas under the pretense of wanting to visit with us and asked Munnie to gather us all up for a visit. Daddy kidnapped us and took us all back to Kansas. He told us that our mother died in the hospital. My siblings told me that we all stayed at the house while Dad went to work. If anyone came to the door, we had to hide, in case it was the police or a social worker.

Munnie got Mother out of the hospital, and the two of them went to Kansas to retrieve us. Mother had to stay there for a few months to prove residency, even though she had the court papers that gave her full custody of us all. When the time was appropriate, she and Munnie took us all back to Houston. Mother went back into the hospital, and Munnie called The Children's Home so they could come get us all.

Foster Care

My first day with the Deardans was memorable. I was three years old, and my brother, Gene, was five. I remember the case worker talking with the Deardans in the living room while Gene and I ate M&M's at the coffee table. I wanted all of the chocolate coated ones while Gene made out like a bandit as I gave him all my colored ones. I didn't understand that all of them were chocolate inside.

We were allowed to call the Deardans Mama and Daddy. They had three teen-aged children, two girls and one boy. Gene slept in the room with Nathaniel, and I stayed in the room with Colleen. Diane had a room to herself.

The house was a two-story with three bedrooms, a bathroom, and a game room upstairs. The lower floor held two bedrooms with a big living room, formal living room, dining room and kitchen. We were not allowed in the formal living room because of all the white carpeting and furniture. It was for entertaining only. It had a two-car garage and a huge backyard. There were trees and beautiful flowers everywhere. To my delight, Daddy put up a rope swing hanging from a tree in the corner of the yard. I would swing forever.

I was so alone without our siblings and didn't understand why I wasn't with them anymore, but Gene tried to assure me that we would see them again. I am told that we got together at Christmas time, but I do not recall this.

The Deardans were really nice and loving people. Daddy told me later that "The Home" told him that he was not to touch me in any way because my biological father had perverted tendencies. I am not sure what they were, but Daddy said that he just couldn't abide by that rule because he knew that I needed a hug and the love of a father. Not just a mother. I have fond memories of lying with Daddy on the couch watching television while Mama read her book at the other end of the couch.

Daddy did a lot with me, from pushing me on a homemade swing in the backyard to teaching me how to crab on the San Bernard River.

I stayed at the Deardans for three years. While at the Deardans home, I can actually say that it was probably the most influential time of my young life. They taught me manners, how to act properly, what love is, and the cruel reality of my life as it was to be.

One of my fondest memories with Mama is making brownies. When eating, I had a bad habit of knocking the food off my plate so I had to scrape it all to the middle before eating. I learned how to set a proper table with all the different silverware. I was so hyper that Mama made me sit on my hands. I was sent to the corner many times. I guess I was not willing to conform.

Mama had grown up in the Bellaire area and remembered my biological mother with her violin case going to school. She often talked about how lonely and homely she looked, and how she always kept to herself. I thought that was cruel, probably because I was like that myself. The Deardans gave me a lot of toys to play with and I had fun with my foster sisters always playing with my hair. I had red hair and freckles. I was so thin, and I sure was a bit gangly looking. Mama told me that when I first came to live with them I was so afraid to lie down in the tub that Daddy had to hold me in the water so she could bathe me. My recollection was that Daddy was trying to drown me. My biological mother told me that I didn't like to sit in the tub, so rather than fight me every night, she just bathed me standing up. With seven kids, I guess she just coped the best way she could. At church, I thought the preacher was Jesus, with his black robes on. My sister, Colleen, told me that was just Jesus' messenger.

The stories I have heard since living there...I guess some were good and some not so good, but all are part of my story. Once, Mama complained that when she volunteered at a preschool, I ran out into the street in front of a school bus while she was gone. She had to quit her volunteer work and stay at home with me instead of leaving me with the maids. I believe she resented me for that. Hey, I was only three, what did she expect? I was a hyper child and needed to be kept busy all the time.

I was able to start kindergarten and liked all the crafts we did. One time the teacher told me to not talk unless I raised my hand first. Well, what does this mean to a five-year-old? I raised my hand and talked away. I got kicked out of school. This was before it was mandatory to attend kindergarten.

They had a house on the San Bernard River outside of Brazoria. We would often go there on the weekends. It was nothing fancy and had a pier that went out over the water, probably about ten to fifteen feet. Daddy once threw me out into the river trying to teach me to swim. It felt as though I was in the middle of the river, but actually only about three feet from the pier. We also did some crabbing. I used to fill up one of those plastic boats with the biggest blue crabs you ever saw. We ate crab forever, it seemed. One time I was trying to get one out of the net and it got loose and pinched me in the knee; a piece of the pincher broke off in it, so the doctor dug it out and now I have a scar from that to this day. I was proud of that scar. I remember showing my battle scar to all my friends.

The Deardans had three kids of their own, but I never felt out of place there. Gene, on the other hand, seemed to always try to please everyone to the point that it became a problem, and Mama told Daddy that it was him or her, so guess who had to leave? I think that Mama got her proper little man in spades. He was very polite, kept his room clean and just wanted to please everyone all the time. Gene went to another foster home. After a year, he went to live on campus of "The Home".

When I graduated from high school, they gave me a party at the river with a few friends, my mother, and stepdad. The Deardans had bought a shrimp boat that summer, and I was going into the Air Force, so I spent a lot of time down there with them and on that boat. Fond memories to add to the bank. By the time I went to basic training, I had a great tan and that was no easy task. I am so fair-skinned that it took a lot of work to not get burnt and just get a tan instead.

Edwards

After three years, I moved in with another family. Their last name was Edwards. I later asked my husband, Dwayne, if he had any family in South Houston. Thankfully he said no. They were not the best people to live with. They had two children of their own and two more foster kids. I remember the other foster girl whose name was Phyllis. She and I slept on bunk-beds in the same room with Mrs. Edwards and her daughter, who slept in the same bed. Mr. Edwards had his own room that was off the boy's room. Nobody was allowed in his room. We weren't allowed to call them Mom and Dad, and they weren't the loving type at all.

They decided to raise rabbits so they made long cages to house the 100 rabbits. The foster kids were made to pick grass for them, and their kids stood over us like overlords. So, as you can imagine, it was us against them. One time, we decided to get back at the Edwards and we, us foster kids, trapped a jack rabbit and put it in the cages with the others. Unfortunately, it killed a few of them. To this day I feel bad about it because we were just hurting the rabbits and not the Edwards so much.

Mrs. Edwards gave us our lunch in a lunchbox with a thermos. You know the kind with a glass liner? I would often ask for her to put ice in mine because I was tired of warm Kool-Aid. One day I tripped getting off the bus and dropped my lunchbox. I didn't realize it, but I had broken my thermos. At lunch, I got it out, and when it shook, I was so excited, thinking that I had finally gotten ice. Needless to say, it was shattered. She thought I had broken it on purpose. Later, I read in our family history reports, that she accused me of breaking it because I wanted a new one.

I really did not like these people. It didn't feel comfortable living there and all I wanted was to see my siblings.

When I left the Deardans, I was only allowed to take a couple of toys with me. I just didn't understand because they had given me so many toys while I was there. The presents at my birthday and Christmas were mine, or so I thought. Phyllis and I only had one place to put our personal stuff, under our bunk bed. One day, the toddler Mrs. Edwards kept was going under my bed to get into my stuff, and she never got onto him for it, so I went under there after him. He bit me and I slapped him. I got in trouble for it. She had also told the case worker that I lied and didn't get along with anyone and was a very problematic child. If I could only give them a piece of my mind now. I was with them for only six months when they lost their license. Why they lost it, I don't know, except that we never went to church which was one of the prerequisites for fostering children through "The Home." I then moved in with my younger sister, Joni, with the Willows.

Willows

I was six and Joni was four. I was so happy to be with her. They also had two children of their own: Robert, a year or two older than me, and an infant, Aiden. This felt like home to me. Mama and Daddy Willows were my new parents. It felt good.

The Willows belonged to Laurenwood Full Gospel Church, now known as Curtis Martin Ministries. Randall Martin was the minister back then and we met in an old feed store. It was a lively church and I didn't quite know what to think of everything I saw. People were speaking in tongues, raising their hands in the air, and passing out. Just strange stuff. We once had a youth minister, Brother Jim. I remember that he was gaining in popularity and was really liked by the youth. Brother Randall got rid of him, and we all thought that it was because he was getting too popular in the church. I heard later that it was for other reasons. I was too young to understand too much back then.

I felt like I needed to belong and Randall Martin always said that you didn't truly believe or accept Christ until you spoke in tongues, so what does a seven-year-old do with that information? Yep, I spoke in tongues. Boy, did I get the attention and I was one with Jesus. I was baptized shortly after that and had become the newest little angel in the church. I didn't realize faking it would bring all that attention. I felt guilty about it, but I was told that now I was walking with Jesus, and that is where I always wanted to be, with my friend, Jesus. After all, I always thought that he was there with me anyway.

There were many late Saturday night gospel services in downtown Houston at Allen's Landing. I remember sitting on a wall, singing and praising God, with people from all walks of life. It was fun and we got to stay out late.

When I first moved in with the Willows, Aiden was about six months old. He was always going into the hospital and coming home with tape on his head; he had water on the brain. He never got better and I guess he was just too weak. He died and there was an incredible sadness all around us. Their faith in God was really the first time that I really witnessed what God was all about. They weren't mad at God at all and explained it to me; Aiden was with God. I was so afraid that they would send both Joni and me away, or at least me.

In later years, Daddy worked as a security guard at the Laurenwood facility. He wasn't allowed to carry a gun, yet on Sundays, Randall had armed police guarding him. One night while at work, he was taken at gunpoint to an empty field and almost shot. Daddy said that he just knelt there, with the gun to his head, and prayed the whole time that God would protect him and forgive this assailant. He let Daddy go back to the church. Daddy's faith was strong and God protected him that time and many other times. How much do we realize how many times God protects us from dangers, seen and unseen?

With three children in the house, two will always gang up on the other. Well, we were no exception. Though we loved each other very much, we were kids. In Monopoly and other games, it would always end up two ganging up on the third. We played and fought like kids; that was really my first experience of how a family really interacted together. We were all in the same age range, unlike living with the Deardans, where their children were much older.

We played with the other kids on the block, catching crawdads in the ditch. We even made a contest out of it to see who could catch the biggest. One time, I found this big daddy of one under a plastic pool in the ditch. He was just lying there. I was so excited to catch this one. We always let them go in the end. After dinner, Mama and Daddy would sit on the front porch while all the kids on the block would play and run around. There are many fond memories of that time.

I remember a Hispanic family down the street where a couple of kids lived. We played with all of them, and their mama made us all tortillas. They were the best treat I could get. Nice and warm. She would hand them out to all of us and we would run off eating and playing again. We had a pretty diverse group of kids of all races. I just didn't know the meaning of segregation or prejudices. I just wanted to be normal and live a happy life.

Taco nights were great. Mama fried up some tortillas and we would chow down. I don't know how many I would eat, but I know I ate a lot. I guess they would be called chalupas. Robert and I would have a contest to see who could eat the most. This was a fun time around the dinner table. Lots of laughing and talking.

We took a trip to a resort one weekend. It was one of those time share programs where they give you a free weekend and try to sell you a membership. It was an adventure, for sure. There was a tornado warning and it was raining like crazy. We had to relocate to another building for safety and Joni and I were scared little girls.

There was a ceramic shack at the end of the street. I would go and buy greenware and clean, fire, and paint it. I really enjoyed doing it, but can't remember what I made or where they wound up. Little did I know that this would be a precursor for a future business venture?

Moving to "The Home"

When I was nine years old, I had to leave. It took me two and a half years to mess this one up, or so I thought. I didn't understand what I had done wrong. Why were they taking me from my sister? I had to go live on campus at "The Home".

My first night, we went to the Ice Capades. I thought it was pretty cool to do something like this. If we did this all the time, it wouldn't be so bad. Not long afterwards, we went to see the Lipison Stallions perform, see a polo match, the circus and several other venues.

On the outside, I guess it looked pretty cool to live there and do all this stuff, but I lived in a cottage with eleven other boys and girls up to age twelve. My brother, Gene, lived in a cottage with ten or so other boys across campus and two of my sisters, Betsy and Annette, were in the "Big Girls" cottage next door. I was not allowed to visit with any of them. We would see each other across the dining hall and just wave. After dinner, we were supposed to go to the gym, but sometimes I would sneak over to my sisters' place to visit with them. I really wanted to spend time with Gene, but they never allowed us to get together and I guess he never pushed the issue either; after all, I was just his little sister.

Just after I went to live at "The Home", they started tearing up the sidewalk to put in a new one for the new gym they were going to build. Some of us were playing in the field, and, low and behold, I got clobbered with a dirt clod, landing square into my nose while I was playing chase with some other children at the other end of the field. I never knew a broken nose could bleed so much. They took me to Hermann Hospital; I was nine at this time, and believe it or not, it was more like a vacation. The nurses were really cool, and my mother was between jobs so she got to spend the night a few times with me. She even bought me some colors and coloring books. I got preferential treatment there. The nurses let me answer the call buttons for the patients when they needed juice or crackers, so I got to visit with some of them, and as long as I stayed on the floor, I got to go where I wanted, not that there was anywhere to go. I never met a stranger, so I made a lot of friends. The Deardans even brought me a mint candy tree. I shared with everyone that came by.

One of the patients there had been in a car accident. She was in a full body cast. I was curious about it. She told me that she had her left leg straight out against the floor of the car. When she had the accident, it slammed her leg bone structure up into her pelvis. Since then, I have never planted my leg straight. It is funny how some things will affect one's actions later in life.

One time, someone donated a batch of blue tennis shoes to The Children's Home. Everyone got a pair, including my sisters. On one of my visits to their cottage, I had to escape through the window to evade discovery and took off with Annette's shoes instead. Needless to say, my feet were larger than hers, so the following morning, I had to go to school with the small tennis shoes on. By the end of the day, they were really hurting, but I couldn't very well tell my cottage mother that I needed to go next door to get my shoes.

We saw a case worker every week or so, I don't remember how often. This person was usually alright to talk to, but I found that nothing ever really got resolved to my satisfaction. Maybe I was just a bit too demanding, like spending time with my siblings or going back to the Willows and my little sister.

When we had to go to the dentist, eye doctor, or physician, there would be a person that would take us; it usually wasn't a caseworker. One time I had the actor that played "Cadet Don" on TV to take me. Cadet Don was a popular children's show that everyone I knew watched. I thought that was so cool. He took me to Alfie's for fish and chips. I thought I was so special.

At Christmas time, all the kids at "The Home" put on a candle light service for family, friends and supporters. We walked in two by two with a lit candle each, singing "Oh Come All Ye Faithful" and wearing white robes. What a bunch of little angels! Yeah right, little did they know! I think we were just lucky that nothing ever caught on fire. After the service, our friends and family came back to our cottages for refreshments, and we could show off our clean and tidy rooms. Now bear in mind that we shared a room with one to three other kids, so imagine how keeping a room neat could be a bit of a challenge, but this day was special, so we all put forth our best efforts.

One year, my dad bought me my own little Christmas tree so I had it tucked into the very small space allotted me for this special decoration. I was so proud of this little Charlie Brown tree. You see, Daddy never found the fullest tree on the lot; in fact, he sought out the Charlie Brown tree they had, so why should my special tree be any exception?

On weekends, when I didn't go home with my parents, we sometimes went to the movies. A couple, the Englemans, would come and load as many kids into the back of their station wagon and haul us to the Garden Oaks Theater. He gave us each a quarter to spend and don't you know, I went after the largest pickle they had in the jar for a nickel and a soda. I think I saw Patton about five times, along with Cat Ballou, and other westerns; I looked forward to the big screen. Unfortunately, that also meant that I missed visits with my mother. She would sometimes call on Thursdays and say that she couldn't come and get me and Joni because she wasn't feeling well. In our later years, I think she finally figured it out that we just wanted to see each other (Joni and I) because Mother never really played with us anyway.

For a period of time, a couple, Mira and Walter O'Banyon, would come and take me to their house for the weekend. They were pretty cool. They took me to the zoo, movies, and just hung out at their house. They seemed to be the most normal couple I'd ever been around, with no kids. I had a great time and enjoyed being with them. I was hoping at some point that maybe they would take me in to be their foster child, but that never happened.

I can't imagine what it is like to not be able to have children. Mira and Walter seemed to really care for me. When I went to church with them, I felt like part of a family again. I really wanted to live with them permanently.

After a time, my mother got jealous and put a stop to it, so I didn't see them much after that until I was an adult. I didn't know if it was something I had done or didn't do. I couldn't understand why they just stopped coming to see me. It wasn't until I was in my forties that I found out why.

While at "The Home", life went on, but with restrictions that I didn't understand, like visitations with my family. I was never allowed a sleep-over with other kids at school. I guess I didn't really have any friends that I can remember, outside of "The Home", but some of the other kids talked about the fun they had at their sleep-over or birthday party, etc. I felt sequestered from the rest of the world. I wanted out of there. At one point, I even started thinking of ways to get out, running away, suicide, getting pregnant, acting totally crazy to get into a hospital or something. I guess a ten or eleven-year-old doesn't think of all the pitfalls.

It wasn't totally bad living there. We did some crafts and played in the gym. We had an art student from one of the local colleges come and teach us some crafts. One time, she showed us how to make silver jewelry. I made a ring out of wax and the instructor took them back to school to pour the silver. Someone stole it at our art show. I remember Annette made a clay sculpture. I got to do some ceramics again. I really enjoyed that the most.
One time, a piano teacher donated her services to teach Annette and I piano. Annette didn't like her too much. The teacher kept telling her to cut her nails. She quit after a couple of months; soon after that, the teacher quit on me. I did learn a little from her.

Pine Tree Camp was a lot of fun. We were usually there for three weeks and our parents would come on the weekends. This was extra special because we could see them more than just the once-a-month visits.

There were three sessions; the first session was for the boys and girls under a certain age, second session was for just girls over a certain age, then the third session was just boys over a certain age. I don't remember the age requirement for each session.

We did all sorts of activities: fishing, swimming, hiking, crafts, singing, and of course, the campfire. For fishing, we had to catch crickets, and then we would go to Spring Creek and fish. I don't really remember catching anything, but it was fun playing down by the creek. After lunch every day, we would gather on the steps in front of the dining hall and sing camp songs, and Poppa Joe would pass out mail. We loved getting mail. The dining hall had a very high-pitched roof so Poppa Joe would toss the letters up to try and get them to sail over the top. Once in a while, he would make it. Then we would go back to our cabins and have a nap.

Swimming was a whole different ball game. In order to swim in the deep end, one had to swim the full length of the pool. On Sundays, when our parents were in attendance, we would get our chance to try out for the deep end. I tried and tried, and finally one day I made it, and Mother was there to see me. I finally made it to the deep end.

One summer, my sister, Betsy, was my counselor. They had a small room off of the main cabin. There was a latch on the outside of their door. I had my bed next to the door and locked the latch so they couldn't get out. I got ribbed for that by my sister. It didn't matter that everyone else was afraid to do it so they egged me on to do it since she was my sister.

Betsy was a good sport about everything, even when Poppa Joe played her singing across the loud speaker during parent's visitation singing "Dem Bones". I remember her running up to the dining hall from way down at the front of the camp. She sang so well and Poppa Joe really admired her. She was always had such a happy-go-lucky attitude.

One summer, when I was at the all-girls session, they played a movie, "I know who you are and I know what you did". They found out that it was not the type of movie to show a bunch of young girls in the middle of the woods. We were all so scared that we doubled up on sleeping arrangements.

There were enough spooky stories at camp that we didn't need a spooky movie too. There was always a story about someone creeping up on the cabins at night and looking in. We had to rake the sand outside of the cabin every day so we would sometimes see footprints behind the cabin and fingerprints on the ledges. This fueled the stories even more.

Going to camp was a chance to get out of "The Home" for a short time. We would load up on the bus and sing songs most of the way there. "When all those Pine Tree Campers fall in line, we're going to have a happy jolly time." It was so much fun. At meals, the set up was much like at "The Home", with each cabin having its own table and two kids helping out in the kitchen, acting as waiters. One time we had grits and there was no apple butter on the table. I can't stand grits and we had to eat a tablespoon of everything.

Adding apple butter to the grits was the only way I could eat them. Ms. Minnie, in the kitchen, came out personally and brought me the apple butter, "I'm sorry about that, Miss Mabelle, I know you need this to get the grits down," she would say to me. She was the head cook at "The Home" and I think she liked me. We all just loved her to death. She was always so sweet to us.

Our family was one of two families at "The Home" that had a large number of kids on campus. Ms. Minnie would always tell me that when the Hynes were all gone, then she would retire because there would be no more kids there that she really loved so much. It was almost true because just a few years after I left, the concept of the living arrangements at "The Home" changed and they were no longer housing as many kids there. Most of the cottages got torn down and there were more satellite clinics for families. All of Houston could get help now.

When I was eleven, my mother got married again, to Irvin. He was alright and had a cool cat. He didn't have any kids and really seemed to love my mother. They had been dating for a while, and we had even spent time with some of his family. Wow, a chance at some normalcy! I had hoped that I'd get to go home as soon as they got married, but that didn't happen, not right away.

At the home, the rooms were set to sleep two or four people. We each had a desk, closet and a drawer. We kept our suitcase above our closet. There were a couple of shelves above the desk for nick-nacs or whatever. We had to keep our space clean and tidy so our cottage parents would come up with inventive ways to keep us interested in keeping it clean. The prizes varied; it could be an extra nickel in our weekly allowance, a choice of what we would hear at nap time, or an extra dessert at dinner one night.

It was not always easy to keep one space tidy with a roommate that was a slob. When I had only one roommate, she and I would get into a fight and start throwing stuff back and forth. It was definitely a challenge. We had a little more room than the room with four, so there was more stuff to throw and more room to keep cleaned up. No matter which room we were in, the bed always went up next to the window. I was afraid of lightning, so I would put my head under the covers until it passed. This is where I really started praying for God to stop being angry and stop the lightning. Gene got to go home to live with Mother and Irvin. I was so jealous. I wanted out of "The Home" so bad. It wasn't until a year later that I went home.

I found out later that they had asked Annette and Betsy to come home first, and they both declined since they would be getting out soon when they turned eighteen. I got to go, and, boy, was I glad. The summer before my sixth-grade, I was tested and found to be dyslexic. When school started, I went to a different school to attend a "Reading Clinic". It was really just a speed reading class. It helped a lot, but I still hated to read and avoided it at all costs. Unfortunately, my grades were not the best in such subjects as English and History.

They required a lot of reading, and I still had trouble comprehending what I read; the teachers weren't all that interesting. It wasn't until I got into high school that I got interested in the subjects because I had teachers that really cared and made the classroom experience interesting enough for me to put forth the effort to do well. I began to really love history.

This elementary school was new for me and I didn't know anyone there. It was also good in a way because nobody there knew that I lived at "The Home", so I wasn't treated like a pariah.

Home for Good

When I started junior high school, after I went home to live, the transition was pretty hard. I guess it was like getting out of jail and suddenly the rules had changed and not necessarily for the better. Irvin was pretty strict, or at least I thought so at the time.

Actually, I was a bit of a loner, and junior high school was pretty hard for me emotionally. I hadn't grown up with the other kids, so I was always the outsider. I only had one real friend, Sue; I knew her from church. I knew only a couple of other children from the previous elementary school I had attended. Gene went there the first year, but he never associated with me at school. I was pretty much a "plain Jane" with glasses and red hair. I had always been ridiculed because of my red hair. My grades weren't too bad, and I did pretty well in most classes. I didn't hang out with any of the "cool" kids or in a "clique".

Gym was especially hard because I hadn't started menstruating yet, and most of the other girls had. I was also pretty much a "carpenter's dream" as the saying goes. I was not well endowed at all, so none of the boys would pay me much attention. I was made fun of all the time. I hated dressing out for gym. Teen-aged girls can be so cruel; boys can too, for that matter.

I had a big crush on a boy named Guy Nelson. He was so cute and popular so all the "cool" kids hung out with him. The kids used to pass notes around in the classroom, you know the kind: Do you like so and so? Check yes or no. Well, one day, Guy passed me such a note: "Do you want to go steady? Check yes or no". Well, of course, I checked "yes". A couple of classes later in the day, he sends me another note to say, "I want to break up." That hurt so bad. I think I cried for days. All the girls, and even Guy, laughed at me for a long time.

When we were at our fifteen-year high school reunion, I think, Guy asked me to dance. While on the dance floor, he asked me to forgive him for that mean trick. He said that he had always remembered that and felt bad about it. I refused at first and made him stew a bit. By the end of the evening, I told him that I forgave him.

I ran into him while I was working in Katy in 2009. He was working as a courier. He was delivering something to my office and heard my name mentioned and asked the front desk if he could see me. I was so surprised. He said that he had become an alcoholic, hit rock bottom and was trying to make something of his life now. It was good to see him, and I think he was genuinely happy to see me.

One of my favorite classes in junior high school was home economics. I loved to cook and sew, and I really liked the teacher. Back then, they taught cooking, sewing, and home management skills like balancing the checkbook and how to shave, just to name a few things. My teacher knew that I loved to sew and said that I showed promise. She brought a tailored jacket she was making for her husband to class; it was made out of suede. She told me that when I could sew something like that with a lining and hand-made buttonholes, then I would be a seamstress.

For my thirteenth birthday, Irvin and my mother sent me to a sewing school. I was to learn how to be a seamstress. The instructor was a nice old German lady. When my dad called, he told her that I could sew very well and wanted me to learn in a formal school. She said that she had heard this many times before, but she very rarely allowed teenagers to take her classes because they didn't stick with it.

I had to audition for the school, and she accepted me. I enjoyed it and loved sitting around the big cutting table listening to her German accent as she told her stories, and gave instruction of course. She would tell me how proud my "papa" was of me.

After I finished the forty hours of instruction, I took a garment back to my home economics teacher and asked her if I passed as a real seamstress. She looked at my dress with the hand-made buttonholes and invisible zipper and so on, and she told me that I was truly a real seamstress and was very proud of my accomplishment. I liked her a lot, so it meant a lot to me to have her approval.

I hated horror shows, and Gene always seemed to watch them with the lights out. I think he enjoyed scaring himself. Gene was a pretty good brother for the most part. He would hear me pecking away at the typewriter, doing my homework, and would sometimes get tired of listening to me, so he would come in and finish typing for me. I did eventually learn how to type 65 wpm. I think I decided that I'd show him.

When my sister, Brenda, got married in Missouri, Mother, Irvin, Gene and I went up to participate in the wedding. She was marrying Ronnie. He was a Seventh Day Adventist. This was an interesting religion with many rules. They were to be married without wedding rings, they didn't drink, eat meat, no coffee and many others. Brenda had red hair, so in some of the pictures, many thought that I was her. I liked to call us seven-year twins, because we were seven years apart. Daddy was supposed to give her away, but he never showed up. I never did find out why. Irvin walked her down the aisle. He was really happy to do it. I think Irvin was more upset that Daddy had disappointed her. Mother made my dress and sewed pearls onto Brenda' dress. I remember sewing being about the only craft Mother and I ever did together.

On the way back to Houston, we passed several turtles. I wanted some, so I had a few of them under my feet in the back seat of the small Pinto wagon. The day after we got back home, Irvin called from work, and he made me set them loose into the bayou. He said that he heard they carried diseases.

When Ronnie and Brenda lived in Louisiana, they would come for visits. They worked as nurses there. I would make a pancake breakfast for everyone. On one of their visits, they told me that they couldn't eat that particular mix anymore. It was made with lard, so they weren't allowed to eat it. This was one of those rules I didn't want anything to do with. They brought a beef substitute that would get hydrated before cooking, so it had to stand for a time. It started smelling really bad. We cooked it up, and it tasted just the way it smelled. We still joke about this. The products have gotten better over the years.

After a time, they moved to Nebraska, then Ohio, and back to Texas. All the siblings finally lived within the state of Texas.

It seemed that Gene and Irvin were always at odds, more so than Irvin and me. Irvin was an alcoholic, so he drank, and from time to time, he would get on his rampage and end up storming out of the house. Once he ran his car into a ditch and messed it up a little bit; that didn't go over well with Mother, of course. I didn't quite understand it all at the time.

Mother had a lot of migraine headaches. One time, she had a monster of a headache and none of the medications would help, so Irvin got the doctor to prescribe a "screwdriver". I think he convinced the doctor to tell her it was ok to have a drink. She never had liquor before in her life. Irvin made the first one with not enough orange juice, so it just made her sick, but when he put in more orange juice, it was ok. Yet when she got better, she told me she was mad because Irvin had ruined her perfect record of not ever having a drink.

Growing up, I remember Mother always took prescription drugs of some sort. She would sit in front of the TV with a newspaper or book, a Coke, corn chips and bean dip. She really never did interact with us. Irvin or I would do most of the cooking, and since we got home before her, it made sense. When I started home economics classes, I was learning to cook, so I did a lot more of the cooking, just to get more practice. I would ask Gene how the meal was and he would just say, "It's eatable," on his way to a second helping.

Dealing with Irvin

I could never talk to my mother about anything sexual or about my body. When the school would send home notes to be signed for me to listen to any sex education films and discussions, she signed with no hesitation because she was never comfortable with talking to me about such issues. Apparently, her mother had taught her that talking about your body was not done and to avoid the issue at all costs.

Just before I came home to live with my folks, I was sort of involved with a boy named Juan Bonita Jr. (JR). It came to be over a situation at "The Home". When I was eleven, a boy took me into the bushes and tried to molest me when JR came along and helped me out of that situation. We became friends because I just couldn't talk about it to anyone. I guess since the boy was seventeen and I was only eleven, I didn't understand what was going on and felt a bit guilty, I think. JR and I hung out together at the gym, and he was the first boy to kiss me. I guess I was twittlepated.

While living at "The Home", JR and I had our lives planned out. We would get married, have three kids and have a nice home. What does a twelve-year-old know about such things? I believe that we just wanted to dream of how we wanted our lives to turn out. When JR moved home, I was so sad and lonely. I felt like I had lost my best friend.

After I went to live at home with Mother, Irvin and I still talked. Once Irvin took me over to JR's house to visit, and he gave me a kitten. I named it Mooch. I got really attached to it because it was my first pet; unfortunately, it had parvo. It died shortly after, and I was devastated.

Not long after that, it got to be too much of an issue for us to get together, and I think I realized that we weren't meant to be, so we broke up. Some years later, he called me and told me that he was happy and getting on with his life and told me that he was gay. I wasn't sure how to take that news.

Gene and I would banter back and forth and mostly he cut me down all the time. It wasn't until later that I would think of a good comeback. I'd think that I'd use it the next time he came at me with that one, but surely, he was so well-versed in cut-downs that he didn't need to use it again, so I was always at a loss. He did get annoying at times. I really loved my brother, and he could be really nice sometimes. We played cards from time to time, and he helped me cope with Irvin's rantings and drinking.

One time, Irvin was trying to stay sober, but he wigged out on us. He ended up in the hospital, and I accused him of drinking. Gene explained to me that it was still in his system, and he appeared drunk, but he would be alright. Mother always got so upset and sad at the situation, but she stuck by him. I thought she was just afraid of being alone with two teenagers again. I know she loved him.

During the summer before I started high school, we moved to another neighborhood not too far away. I liked the new place; it was larger than the last. I was now starting to blossom a little and felt better about myself. I wanted a job, but I was still only fifteen, so Irvin told me to go ahead and lie about my age because they couldn't afford to give me money for Christmas shopping or much else, so that is what I did. I went to work down the street at a Weiner's. Unfortunately, when I started school, the manager's nephew was in my driver's education class, so he knew how old I was. He told his uncle who called me into his office and told me that he couldn't keep me on, but when I turned sixteen, I could come back and he'd hire me back. I felt awful and cried the three blocks home. When I told Irvin, he just said, "Well you should not have lied to him." I wanted to smack him.

I enjoyed my classes and teachers. Of course, I was boy-crazy by now, but didn't really start dating much until the tenth grade. I did date a boy from a church that our youth group did a musical with. I came out of my shell and became more confident. I still hated my name, and when I started driver's education, I tried to start going by my middle name, Juanita, but a boy in there knew me as Mabelle, so Juanita didn't stick. I guess I didn't exactly look like a Juanita. Being a white girl with red hair, I just couldn't pass as a Juanita.

Irvin and I did some father-daughter stuff that I guess we would really call father-son stuff. We went fishing and crabbing at the coast. One time, we caught some croakers. They really do croak. When we got home, we told Mother about the fish croaking, then Irvin said that catfish meow too. She really didn't believe us then about the croaker. We all laughed like crazy.

Irvin, being the alcoholic, he was, would take me for my "driving lesson" every weekend, and of course, the first stop was the local convenience store for a beer or three. We'd go driving all over. At that time, I was dating Dwayne, now my husband, so we would drive over to his house. I would go in and visit with Dwayne and Irvin would sit outside drinking his beer.

For a while before I left home, Irvin had a motorcycle. It was pretty cool. He would take me out on it once in a while. I thought that was funny because I dated a guy with one and Irvin griped about me being out on it with Ray. Irvin later sold his after having an accident and almost killing himself. I think he was drunk and rolled down the embankment of the freeway. I guess Mother made him get rid of it; after that, he bought a big truck. This was after I left to go into the Air Force.

When I was about seventeen, I was dating a guy and Irvin would follow us. I hated that. I guess he just didn't trust me, and I didn't know how to get him to. I confronted him about it, and of course he denied it, but he drove a yellow Honda Civic, which was pretty unmistakable. I was mortified, but my date had a good sense of humor and gave Irvin a run for his money. We lost him after a bit. I think my date liked the excitement.

My first experience with the seriousness of some illnesses was when Sue, my best friend, and probably my one true friend, took ill. She ended up with a colostomy and went through hell with all the restrictions and embarrassment. Fortunately, she healed up well. The

colostomy was reversed, and all was well. I was scared. I
didn't want to lose anyone else, and she was my lifeline
to sanity.

Daddy

My younger sister, Joni, would visit us once a month for the weekend. I enjoyed having her there. We could talk and play around together. When we had to go visit with Dad on the first Sunday, I really just liked spending the time with Joni. Dad was so old-fashioned and lived like he was in the dark ages. He wouldn't have central air, a television, or a good working refrigerator. When the refrigerator went out, he would just buy a block of ice and put it in the bottom. The milk was just barely cool, and I hated it. Joni would about gag, so I would try to drink most of it for her, so Dad didn't yell at her. Or I would just dump it out the window when he wasn't looking. He did some pretty abnormal stuff like putting the pilot light of the stove on high and put the pot of potatoes on to boil it. They would be done by the time we got home from church.

He used to make Joni and I walk around the yard and pickup sticks for the grill. Even when there wasn't much, he would yell at us to pick up even the smallest pieces. I used to think he was just too cheap. Nowadays, I pick up sticks, but I still buy charcoal. I do love to smoke on my grill though.

When we were little, we were not allowed to spend the night with Dad. It wasn't until I was about ten, I guess, that Joni and I could spend the night. Looking back at some of the things Dad did, I guess he might have been a little off?

Dad drove like a mad man. He would laugh out loud at restaurants and embarrass us. He tried to show us a good time, but I think he was just too much out of tune with current parenting. He didn't know what we wanted to do, and we didn't know how to act with a parent, I guess. He had a few old school desks in one room that we all took turns sharing when we visited. He made us write letters to our grandparents and aunts and uncles. I guess that was good, but we didn't know them, so it was hard to talk to someone we'd never met.

Daddy was a Christian man and believed that all our troubles would be solved if we went to church. He failed to tell us how. For a while, he went to the First Methodist Church in downtown Houston. Right after he would drop Joni and I off at our class, we would take off and walk around downtown. It was like we were escaping on our own adventure. We had a blast, and as long as we were back to meet Dad at his class on time, we were ok.

To stave off the boredom during the service, he would make us little rag dolls out of his handkerchief. Whenever we would eat out, he was so diligent in tipping everyone, including the ones refilling the tea glasses twenty-five cents.

Sometimes, he would take Joni and I to the beach. Once, he took most of us kids at one time. I don't remember who all went, but he did barbeque on the beach, and when he finished, he dumped the coals out onto the sand. I was real young at the time and thought they needed to be covered up. Joni didn't see them and stepped on them, burning her feet. I felt awful. Daddy put butter on the burns, which we now know you should never do. Other than that, we all had a good time. I think I just enjoyed being with some of my siblings. I didn't care where we were.

Daddy tried to get us all at Christmas. That was the one time we could all see each other. Sometimes, Mother got us all for another celebration around Christmas time. Daddy made us all sing Christmas Carols. I think he thought we were the Von Trapp family. We actually sounded pretty good. Gene was in the Houston Boys' Choir for a while when he was young. He had a beautiful voice. He still carries a tune pretty well.

The one constant with Daddy's Christmas celebrations and something we all remember and still laugh about was his Christmas trees. He always found the "Charlie Brown" tree. It never was a pretty one, and usually he cut it down himself out of some lonesome forest somewhere. He would decorate it with icicles made out of sardine can twists and paper ornaments.

After Christmas, he would cut off most of the branches and use it as a hat rack for the rest of the year.

I sometimes hated visiting with him, and even asked my mother, after I moved home, if I still had to go. Of course, I had to; I really wanted to just see Joni and didn't feel right leaving her alone with him and his abnormalities. Not to mention, she would not have very much fun.

I have to hand it to him, though. He always tried to live in a house somewhere close to us, so we had a home we could go to when things got bad. He worked clear on the opposite side of town, so I know it was a bit of a trip to get to and from work, but he wanted to be as close to us as he could.

I heard in later years that when Daddy and Mother got divorced, Daddy tried to get his siblings to take some of us so he could keep us with family, if possible. Unfortunately, they couldn't because of their lives and situations.

When Daddy moved out to Hockley, he was not too active in community activities. I knew he loved to play 42, so I convinced him to come with me to the Hockley Community Center under the pretense that I needed to check it out for potential customers for my ceramic shop. I knew that they had activities for seniors and wanted to get his interest piqued.

We went and checked it out. On Fridays, they had a lunch and played dominoes and cards. He was hooked. He played every Friday for years, until his fall.

I tried to have some type of a relationship with Dad over the years, and I guess we just didn't know how. He was stuck in his time period and refused to accept that women could be in a successful career and do almost as much as men.

When I joined the Air Force, I had to deny that I knew where he was because I had to get his signature on my delayed enlistment forms. I knew that he would never sign. He would tell me how it was a "dog's life" and didn't understand why I wanted to go into the service. He just didn't get it. I hated to read and was not college material.

When Dad went into the Army, a woman married him for the insurance and served him with divorce papers before he even got off the train upon his return. She thought he would die in the war, and she would get his insurance. I guess he got pretty bitter about the whole thing after that. He never talked about his experiences. Once, I did get him to tell me a little, but overall, he hated the time he served. I asked him one time for his ribbons and medals from the Army, and he told me that I could get them when he died because they didn't mean anything to him. I wanted to make him a shadow box to display them.

One time, I tried to open my life up to him and told him that I was planning to go into the Air Force Reserves and cross train into On-Board Weapon's Control Systems. It would mean going to Mississippi for three months. I had just gotten my ceramic business going and hated to lose the momentum I was experiencing and leave the family behind. Dwayne said that he could come out there from time to time with the kids, and it would be alright if that is what I really wanted to do. Daddy listened to all I had to say and seemed to be alright with my decision; we talked a bit. I felt that maybe this was a start to a relationship. However, when I got home after that visit, Daddy called and blasted me for wanting to get another career under my belt, and my place was to encourage Dwayne and his career. I needed to stay at home and raise the family, not run around and do more training. He just didn't get it. Dwayne and I had worked it all out, but it was still uncertain if I would even go back into the military anyway. I decided not to go because Clinton was elected and utilized the reserves more extensively. Dwayne did have a problem with me getting into a battle zone, so I decided not to go. I never opened up to Daddy again.

We were never really friends. He was in his 40's when I was born, and he and my mother were more like grandparents than parents. They weren't exactly fun-filled folks.

Dad was a balding, thin man that took pride in how well he could live in poverty. I think he was born in the wrong century. Being the male chauvinist that he was, I couldn't have any sort of civil conversation with him about the careers I chose. He thought that I should not be the one to do the home building, plumbing or anything that a "man" should be doing. This will always be a "man's" world to him.

When I joined the Air Force, he threw a fit when he found out that I was going to be a Jet Engine Mechanic. "That's a dog's life," he would rant. I went anyway, but unfortunately, I got the job as a plumber. That really got dad's goat.

In 1993, we started looking to move into the same area as Dad. I wasn't exactly looking forward to living too close to him, but the area was high in elevation. Dad started looking with the local real estate brokers to find us some property. I started taking house building and residential superintendent classes at the local college. We were on our way to getting our first house.

After taking the construction finance class, I realized that we needed a lot more money than we had to be able to build our own home, so we started looking for an existing house.

Dad's Last Days

In 1994, Dad fell, broke a hip, and wound up in ICU. He had told me earlier that year that he wanted to get married again. Later, he changed his attitude about the church he was going to as well as going to his usual Friday domino game at the community center. I wasn't sure what it was all about until he broke his hip. I had a bad feeling when he went into the hospital. After surgery, he was more cantankerous than usual. He was throwing the ice bags into the hall and refusing the breathing treatments. The surgery went fine, except for a short bout with pneumonia. He improved so they moved him into rehab. Not long after he was there, the pneumonia came back bad, and he wound up in ICU.

The family set up camp in the ICU waiting room. I was in the middle of taking classes, and of course, everyone was working, so we all took turns sitting at the hospital. It felt like we lived up there. In spite of his faults, we all respected the fact that he was our father, and he tried the best he could to keep the family as close as possible. He did the best with what he had.

One time, I got so mad at him for wanting to drive (he was legally blind), that I told him the truth about my feelings for him. I told him that I didn't have the love for him that a daughter should have for a father because we never could relate as a father and daughter should. I know that it hurt him, but I was so worn down by the attitudes he gave me; he wouldn't converse with me like a father should. He acted like a dictator and showed no respect for me or my decisions in anything I did. There was never a middle ground with him, only his way, so I stopped trying to talk with him on a general conversation level.

Well, there we sat in the waiting room and all of us are talking about anything and everything. One time, Gene had been to Dad's house and read his journal.

Gene said, "You should read his journal; he was talking so weird." So, the next time I went out there, I did read his journal. Gene was right, but now I began to realize why he had given up and talked the way he had about church and the community center. He had told a woman from church that he wanted to marry her. She told him that she was not interested in him in that way. This must have crushed him because he was writing stuff like, "Lord, please help this woman find her way" and "I can't continue to be on this earth…". He had given up on life and this is why he was in the ICU.

Joni got so upset with me for reading Dad's journal. "What are you doing reading someone else's private feelings? You had no right," she admonished. Dwayne told her, "You shouldn't write anything down that you don't want someone to read someday."

As the days went by, we all learned a little bit about each other. I was listening to Joni and Betsy talking about our older brother, David. I had known for quite some time that he had wanted a sex change operation. I dealt with it a long time ago. David had been into drugs since 11th grade and didn't live a very good life. He lied, cheated, and stole from the family for years, and I didn't want anything to do with him once I was married and had my own problems.

Joni did not help with his errands, like taking him to the doctor or store. Instead, she would call him on Thursdays and prayed with him and helped him work on his family journal, which he wanted to put together. She was our prayer warrior. She had her way of dealing with dad in her life, as we all did. I lived closest to him, only 27 miles, so I went pretty often.

Joni and Betsy were talking about a different side of David that I never got the chance to see before he died in 1983. He was found dead in the YMCA the day after I moved home from Wyoming. I didn't even know he was in town. They thought that he was gay, but I know that men wanting a sex change were not gay. Tears started to come, and they looked at me like I was nuts.

"Mae, what's wrong," they asked. All I could get out was "gay?" They thought for sure I was off of my rocker. Joni wondered what turnip truck I'd gotten off of, not knowing this about David. She thought I had a problem with him being gay. Later, I told her that just because David wanted to change his sex did not mean that he was gay. She and I had not been close in a long time, and this made it worse.

By midweek, Dad was on life support for good with no hope of recovery. By this time, he was not coherent and failing. We had to accept the fact that he was dying. He seemed to hang on though; that's how stubborn he was. Some of our ministers came up with us for comfort, and I was having a hard time the day that the doctor told Betsy and I that he was not going to come out of this. My minister, Dan, talked with us and said that one belief was that the loved one sometimes felt that they can't leave without knowing their loved ones were going to be all right. Maybe they need to know that they are dying, and it's ok to move on.

Dan and I went in to see my dad and the hardest thing I have ever had to do was to tell Dad that he was dying. I couldn't do it at first, and tears streamed down my face. We prayed with Dad; afterwards, I told him that he was dying, but it would be ok because he would be in heaven with David and his relatives. I told him that his children would be all right, and we'd have each other. I went back into the waiting room where Betsy was and told her that I told him. I was still crying, but I felt better, knowing that he could now move on in peace.

By the end of the week, it was just a matter of time, so my aunt flew in from Kansas City. She had just lost her husband the year before, after a long illness in the hospital. She had to deal with it all by herself and really didn't want to see Dad alive and just hanging on. After I picked her up from the airport, she said she changed her mind. She hoped that he would hang on long enough for her to see him.

On the way to the hospital, there was a truck stuck under the overpass at the freeway, which was just down from the hospital. I had a four-wheel drive truck, and we were sitting beside a construction area, so I just hopped the curb and went through the construction. We got beyond the tie up and made it to the hospital in an indirect route. All the while, Aunt Betty was so funny. As we were driving through the construction, I told her "have truck will travel" and she was making out like we were inspecting the site.

We got to the hospital and went in to see Dad for a few minutes. Aunt Betty told us all to go home for a break and shower, to relax and spend time with our families. She would call if there was any change. I pulled into the driveway of my house, and my husband said that Aunt Betty called and Dad's breathing was very labored. This was it. We showered and Dwayne and I went back up to the hospital.

We all gathered in his room together. I was standing next to the monitor hand in hand with my siblings and aunt. We prayed and sang "How Great Thou Art". This was one of the songs we sang, but never got quite right. But we'd have to give it a try. Towards the end of the song, his heart rate dropped, but didn't stop; we didn't get it right again.

"I guess he needs one more song," I said as I looked up and noticed that he was still hanging in there. So we sang "Amazing Grace" and got it right. I looked at the monitor and noticed that his heart stopped just as the last note was sung. A beautiful peace settled on him and we all cried and waited for the nurse to come in. Unfortunately, the breathing machine could not be shut off until a doctor came and pronounced him dead. It seemed too cruel to have it continue just one second longer, but those are the rules.

After he died, I did get some of his Army stuff, and from his discharge papers, I was able to purchase replacements for some of the medals that were lost or Joni wouldn't give me at the time. After I got a hold of most of them, I made little shadow boxes with Daddy's picture in uniform and a few of his medals and ribbons and gave them to each of my siblings. I made a big one with all the ribbons and medals and his flag for myself and displayed it proudly.

After Daddy's death, Joni took the journal and made a book out of it. She added all her impressions and visitations from the family and so on. Betsy's and my entries were more medical since we have a medical background. We tried to just relay the pertinent information to everyone else. Joni decided to add her prayers and commentary to this book. I received my copy of it the day before Dwayne and I were heading up to North Carolina for his grandmother's funeral. I put it in the truck to read as we drove.

David

I had my experiences with David when I was in high school. He would call and get Mother and Irvin to send a bus ticket under the pretext that he would get off drugs and go into rehab. So he came to Houston and went into rehab numerous times. He even started getting his life together, or so we thought, but one Christmas, he stole my brand-new tape recorder. He said that he was wanting to borrow Gene's, but he wasn't home, so I let him take my new one that I had just gotten for a Christmas present from Mother and Irvin. David left Houston and my tape recorder went with him. Irvin was so mad. Every time David would call, he would tell me that he would send it back to me, but never did; so one time Irvin told us that we were not to accept any more collect calls from him until he returned the recorder. I think Irvin had lost his patience with David, and I can't say I blame him. I had lost all faith in my brother over that and all the lies that he would straighten out his life.

When I got married and entered the Air Force, I had problems enough with my marriage, so I asked the family not to tell David where I was. He had a habit of calling collect and talking someone into bailing him out of jail or letting him live with them. He would take off, with our property and leave behind a large phone bill. I didn't need that. Not that I didn't love my brother, but I couldn't deal with his problems since I had enough of my own.

Once while I was in high school, I received a call at home from a counselor from California, wanting to talk with David's family. I told her that I was his sister. She explained to me that David was trying to get a sex change operation and wanted my impressions of his mental state and his relationships with the family. I had no idea of what was going on with David. Mother confirmed that these were David's wishes. She didn't want anything to do with the situation, but still loved David regardless.

David never got the operation, but I guess he was always upset with being stuck with a man's body. He had confided to Mother that he used to wear my sister's clothes when he was younger and had to go to a resale shop to purchase men's clothing for the trip to Houston.

I have known a few men that wanted, and some that have received, the gender reassignment operations. It was a brutal treatment, and they really had to go through hell during the process. They were not gay and explained it to me this way: A gay man doesn't want a man that has become a woman, and a lesbian woman doesn't want a woman that was once a man. A man that wants to be changed into a woman just wants to become what they feel inside, a woman. They want a relationship with a man who wants a woman; therefore, no homosexual behavior is involved, as far as they are concerned.

David was thirty-two when he died, but my family said that he looked to be in his late forties. I just couldn't go to his viewing. I wanted to remember him the way I last saw him.

Hamilton Junior High School

Junior high school was an eye opener. I started finding out how other kids really acted, and it wasn't all good. I was sheltered from a lot of the abuse they inflict upon each other. At "The Home", we were not allowed to verbally abuse each other. We had structure in our lives, and now I didn't have that structure. It took some getting used to. The girls were mean sometimes, and one in particular was really mean, ambushed me after school and beat me up. She knocked my glasses off and kept on swinging. All of that over what someone else told her I said about her. It wasn't true, but she never gave me a chance to defend myself. I didn't know how to fight and was totally upset about how to handle the situation. I tried to be nice and respectful to everyone and couldn't believe that someone would say such things about me. I think it was a girl that was jealous of me because I was making friends with some of the girl's friends while playing volleyball in gym class.

I did my best in my classes and studied hard because I still had trouble comprehending what I read, so it took me longer to do my homework. I loved math and excelled in it. Sometimes a few kids would ask if they could copy my work; I refused, so they would start making fun of me. I just didn't understand why they acted as they did. Irvin would just tell me they were jealous. I sure didn't feel like I was anyone to be jealous of.

I would walk to and from school most days. When Gene started high school, I walked home alone. Once in a while, I had someone to walk with, but most of the time, I was alone. For however long it took me to get home, I had time to think. Boy, what a mistake. I would grumble to myself about all that was wrong in my life. I hated the arguments with Irvin and his drinking. It seemed that he liked to yell. I hated it, so I would retreat into my own world.

Mother and Irvin took me to church every week which I really enjoyed. We belonged to Grace United Methodist Church in the Heights. I was a member of the MYF, Methodist Youth Fellowship, and made some good friends there. Most of my best childhood memories were associated with church and always wanted my kids to get some of that, but unfortunately, they didn't and turned away from the church. I know that one does not have to go to church to be a Christian, but the church can be a wonderful resource for spiritual growth. I have found that my church family can be very uplifting.

I looked forward to MYF all week long. At least there, the other kids were nice to me, and we all enjoyed time together. I became an officer in the MYF, and I really felt accepted. I was a tomboy and played football, even in my brand-new skirt outfit. That really made Mother and Irvin mad. I just didn't get that a girl doesn't play football in a skirt. Gene attended MYF, as well, and was either nice to me or ignored me. At least he wasn't mean.

In the summer time, we attended a church camp called Lakeview. I really had a blast and loved to help the arts and crafts instructor. A few years later, she asked me to take over the arts and crafts. I did and later became a counselor once I was old enough. I would get all kinds of laughs when I would show up to lunch with purple or green hands from our tie die projects.

After I started high school, I met a boy at camp named Tom Shell. He could play any instrument put before him. He was funny, and I thought the moon rose and set by him. We became pen pals and wrote to each other for years. I just couldn't understand why he never asked me out. I was just so upset when year after year, he would hook up with another girl while at camp. At the end of the week, we would hug and say our goodbyes and continue to write throughout the year.

One year at camp, I met a boy, and we hit it off. We hung out together all week. His name was Steve. He drove a station wagon and lived south of Houston. I was seventeen at the time and had fun with him. He was nice, funny and got along great with everyone. He asked me out and wanted to take me out when we got back after camp. He drove some of the kids back to their church in Houston and came over to my house. Since he lived out of town, I told him he could take a shower at my house since we were going out that evening. Irvin came home after work while Steve was still in the shower. He blew a gasket. I understand it now, but back then, I just didn't understand Irvin's anger at my bringing a boy over to my house when they weren't home to take a shower. I didn't realize it was just not appropriate. I thought that since I had spent all week with him and he was involved with church, it was alright and I trusted him.

Steve took me to a really nice restaurant. It was so romantic. He was such a gentleman and drove me home afterwards. We spoke from time to time, but never went out again. Long distance relationships just don't work out well.

Gene and Irvin were never getting along, it seemed, and Gene moved out to live with Daddy. One condition for him to move out was that he had to still pick me up and take me to school, so I wouldn't have to ride the city bus.

Waltrip High School

Gene told me when I first started high school that I was to get out of the car immediately upon arrival and was not to acknowledge him in the hallway. He was ashamed of me, I guess. I wasn't cool like him and his buddies.

Once when Joni and I were visiting with Daddy, Gene made a comment that he and Joni could double date sometime when she started dating. I told him that I was dating some. He told me that there was no way he would go on a date with me. That hurt me terribly. I knew then that he was really ashamed of me and really didn't want anything to do with me. I adored my brother and he could have cared less about me. The world can really be cruel. So can brothers.

I met some kids in JROTC and saw what they were doing. I thought it was cool that they could shoot guns and learn all that military stuff. It intrigued me. I started thinking about it and did some research. I found out that if I took three years of JROTC, I could go into the military with rank. I knew that I was not college bound. That wasn't for me, so I decided that I would join the Air Force. All of our classes were split up into two quarters, so if I took JROTC all three semesters both in 11th and 12th grade, it would count as three years' worth. I talked to the guidance counselor about it, and with much ado, I convinced everyone that I was serious, and they approved it.

JROTC was a big part of my life, and I became a lieutenant and in charge of the drill team. I loved rifle drill and going to competition. I became an expert Marksman and was even chosen from our school to compete for Citywide Outstanding Cadet. This was an Army level award, so it was nice to be chosen, but I studied like crazy anyway. I competed and won first place. At the year-end ceremony, I was awarded a plaque, ribbon and medal. It was so cool. I felt like I had really accomplished something big.

At one point, all the girls were tired of the old uniforms so we petitioned and got permission to make our own. I ended up making all of them. They were blue slacks and vest. I think we looked pretty sharp. So we were able to wear them at competition.

High school was actually fun most of the time. I was really out of my shell by now, but I decided that I was just going to have fun and get school over with. I really liked my classes, and I had a great homeroom teacher. He talked me into joining the photography club when he found out that was one of my interests. My friend David was the only other member, but that was alright because he taught me how to use the dark room and do all kinds of developing tricks with black and white film.

One of our trips with the scuba club to Canyon Lake was an experience I didn't care to repeat. Some of us got drunk and I fooled around with one of the boys and got in trouble. Irvin found out and wanted to bring charges against the boy even though nothing really happened, but Irvin was determined. That was when I discovered he had been reading my diary. In my diary, I embellished a bit and Irvin accused me of sleeping with the guy. I accused him of reading my diary because that was the only way he'd know; of course, he denied it. I suspected he had been reading it all along. So much for his telling me that writing in it was the best way to express disappointments and joys, but it would be my private way of dealing with issues that I didn't want to talk to anyone about. Needless to say, that boy wouldn't have anything to do with me again after that.

Mother and Irvin were always going to counseling and thought that it would be a good idea if I went. My problem was just your normal problems with any parent. I was having problems making Irvin understand that trust goes both ways. He didn't trust me out on dates, and I didn't trust him not to take a drink. I'm sure that we all had a time with adjustments. Mother wanted us home I'm sure of it, but she didn't know how to deal with being a mother. She didn't want to address issues that needed to be addressed, such as dating, discipline or chores. She just wanted to exist, without making any of the decisions around the house. I just wanted her to step up to the plate and make a stand one way or the other to show me she cared.

My mother was a smart person and very well read. She read all the time. I think she liked to escape into a book instead of dealing with reality. She was addicted to prescription drugs. She had to go into the hospital a couple of times to get the dosages regulated after flipping out on them, especially the pain killers. Once I started my cycle, I only had a few per year, and when I did, I was in so much pain that she was ready with the Darvon or Valium. I had to stay home from school sometimes, not so much from the pain, but the drugs made me a little loopy.

One episode, while Mother was in the hospital, Irvin and I were home; he was drinking. He started making advances towards me. I was scared as he chased me around the house, and I ran out and managed to call Sue's dad to come over. I wanted to stay with my sister Betsy, but they called Mother at the hospital; she decided it was best I stay with the preacher. I just wanted to get out of the house and be with my sister. I didn't think Mother was being fair.

My relationship with Irvin was not the same and very strained for some time to come. Back into therapy we went. I don't remember much about it, but it was a long time before I trusted Irvin again.

During my senior year in school, Tom Shell came to our church as Youth Director. I was so happy. I thought this was my chance to finally win him over. Well, I don't know if I was trying too hard or not hard enough. I finally gave up when he asked out the preacher's daughter, Kathy. I was so mad and jealous. I was due to go into the Air Force that summer and decided to heck with all of them. My friends Sue and Greg and I hung out the rest of the summer at church functions and to heck with Tom and Kathy.

A few days before I left for basic training, my friend Dale came over to say his goodbyes. He had dated Sue, but told me how he had wanted to date me too, but didn't want to hurt Sue since we were best friends. He planted a big kiss on me and left. What a day.

The day before I left, Tom came by, and we talked a good long time. He told me how sorry he was for letting me go and that he now realized what he had missed out on. He just never gave me a chance. He kissed me and said he wanted to continue to stay in touch. We did for some time.

Joni

I just don't know where I went wrong with our relationship. Joni and I had been close at one time, and I regretted that we weren't anymore. Once, when Joni was visiting, my friends and I wanted to go to the "Rocky Horror Picture Show". Mother and Irvin let her go with us. She was sixteen and figured she was old enough. I really don't think that they knew what it really was. My friends, Dale, David and I went to the show a lot of times.

It was the current cult craze and all the teenagers were going to the midnight show. We went to a bar before the show; Joni didn't drink alcoholic beverages, of course. We went to the movie and sat in the balcony in the back row. If you've ever seen this movie, you'd know that is significant because it is mentioned in one of the songs in the show and there is audience participation. We were all waiting for her reaction, when she saw Dr. Frank-N-Furter come off the elevator and throw off his cape revealing a corset. Not to make fun of her, but she had led such a sheltered life and not knowing what this was all about, her expression was priceless. We all had fun though, and she started to get into the groove of the show. We sang along with the rest of the audience during certain parts of the movie and of course there is the dance, "The Time Warp".

When Joni went home to the Willows, I guess she told them all about her weekend, and I don't know if they were shocked or she didn't really like it or not, but Mrs. Willows didn't like me picking Joni up in my car and started to refuse Mother's access to Joni unless she picked her up.

I wanted to have more time with Joni, but I wasn't allowed to do anything with her by myself after that. I joined the Air Force the summer after high school, so I wasn't around for her and felt bad sometimes, but it couldn't be helped. I didn't get any return mail from her; I guess I just gave up when I started having problems with my marriage, which was pretty soon after moving to Guam.

Meeting Dwayne

During the summer of 1976, I went to the beach with my sister, Betsy, Dwayne, and friends. I went riding around the beach with Dwayne and his friend. We started dating after that. I found out later that it was Betsy's intention to introduce us so that maybe we would start dating. Betsy was living with Faith's family for a bit after she returned home from Oklahoma until she got on her feet. I can honestly say that my sister lived with my husband before I did.

We dated for about nine months. He went to a different school than I did, so we just saw each other on the weekends. Some dates, he would take me downtown and skateboard. I should say that he skateboarded. I just walked around with him. One time he had borrowed his mother's car when someone broke into it and stole my wallet. I think he felt worse about it than I did.

Sometimes we would go to the park on Allen Parkway, near downtown. It was a nice park with green grass, and across from it was the Holiday Inn. It had a neon green sign. We would just lay on the grass and talk and look at all the lights in and on the buildings around us.

One time, I asked him to pick out a movie that I would treat for his birthday. He picked "If You Don't Stop It You'll Go Blind". Within the first ten minutes, he was embarrassed about going to a movie like that with a girl. He didn't know what it was about when he chose it. We went out to eat after the movie.

I really liked Dwayne and I think he liked me. We went to movies, both inside and drive-ins, and hung around his house and watched movies on the television. He really liked watching movies.

After just nine months, he told me that he had too much going on with school and work and he really didn't have time to date right then. We stopped seeing each other, but I never stopped liking him.

When I was about to graduated high school, he called and asked me out. We went out and it was nice, but I was leaving shortly for the Air Force and he had other plans than dating me.

Joining the Air Force

In 1978, I was sworn into the Air Force. I had a guaranteed job as an jet engine mechanic. I was due to leave and had to take my final physical. I answered one of the questions wrong and got delayed. So, I lost my job and instead went in under open field mechanical. That means that they can choose whatever job they have open for you. As it turns out, I really could have kept it if the system worked right. After bypassing most of basic training, I would have been going to job training at the original appointed time had I gone earlier. Oh well. I got picked to be a plumber.

Basic training was interesting. I took the bus from Houston and landed in San Antonio at Lackland AFB. I was used to the Army lingo and not too sure of what the ranks were in the Air Force. My drill instructor (DI) was a red head as was her assistant and twin sister. My first-time reporting to her was, well, let's say frustrating. I knocked on her door, marched in and stood at attention in front of her desk. She asked me if I was forgetting something. We repeated this a few times with my not understanding what I was leaving out. Finally, she told me I was forgetting to salute. I made the biggest mistake by telling her that I didn't salute non-commissioned officers. She had it in for me from then on.

During basic training, I was awarded the rank of Airman First Class, which is the second level of rank (E2). I was not able to put on my stripes for a while afterwards though. I already knew how to drill and other aspects of the military training that we had to learn. We took classes like Military Law, where one of our classmates found out that the drill instructors were not allowed to touch us. This girl had turned eighteen during training and thought she was a tough girl. She brought charges on our DI. So, she and her sister were taken from us, and the assistant DI from our mother flight came to us along with another man as the assistant. Previously my DI would not allow me to bypass basic training, but now with the new

DI, he would sign off for me to bypass as long as I passed all inspections. He wanted to finish out his first flight, so he spent most of his time with them, and his assistant stayed with us. I was finally able to get my stripes and move on to finishing basic training.

As part of our training, there were big drawings of officers and non-commissioned officers mounted to the pillars under our barracks. This was for us to practice on who we were to salute. One time I was walking around and some newbies saluted me. I turned around to see if there was an officer behind me. I saluted back, but laughed my fanny off. They just didn't get it yet. I had to go through the obstacle course with a male flight. I made it, but really wanted to qualify with the M16 rifle. At that point, it was not mandatory for women to do so. Later, I found out that just after I left, they did make it mandatory. I had missed my chance.

At tech school in Wichita Falls, TX, we were finally able to go by our first names. I saw this as my chance to get rid of "Mabelle" and remembered Daddy Deardan calling me his Mae-Mae. So that is when I became "Mae".

I was up at 4 a.m. and marching off to class across the flight-line. I was in a class with nine men and a male instructor. For the first two hours of class, everyone was trying to wake up. I would go walk around the halls for a bit. One time, I came back in time to hear the end of a dirty joke. The guy turned red as my hair. I told them that I had a joke, and that was all it took. They didn't have to wait for me to leave to start the joke fest. I heard some pretty dirty jokes, but don't remember but one or two.

I was paired up with the shortest guy in class. Our goal was to finish a mock bathroom with ground up construction and a water heater without leaks. We learned all sorts of plumbing, and I had a time trying to remember the names of the tools. After a few "thingamagig, doohickies and doomaflochies", the instructor handed me a book with drawings of all the tools and told me that he didn't want to hear "thingamagig, doohicky or doomaflochy" again. I learned pretty quickly.

One time, we had to cut a six-inch cast iron pipe with a chain cutter. It was a sight to behold. My partner was on the ground pulling and I was on top pushing down on this lever type of tool trying to make the cut. Needless to say, the other classes were all watching with such amusement. We got it cut and a few more as well. Picture day was a hoot. With me being the photo bug, I suggested a special pose. With so many men with me, it had to be me on the throne (toilet) and my subjects all around me. I had a roll of copper tubing as my halo. By the time we were done with the class, I was an experienced plumber and knew the names of all the tools; we only had a couple of leaks, which we corrected and passed. Our bathroom was complete. I had been accepted into the male plumbers' elite.

One of the things we had to do with training was go down a manhole. Yea, you guessed it; the guys shut the lid on me. I freaked out for about half a second. They thought they were so funny.

While at tech school, I had dated a few guys and one in particular, Tim. He was a plumber as well, and in the class just ahead of me. He was seventeen, and I was eighteen. We hit it off, and he decided that he wanted to marry me. I kept saying "no". At one point, I went home for the weekend and tried to reconnect with Dwayne just to see if it was a done deal. I guess it had to be because I just couldn't find him. So, upon my return to base, Tim asked me one more time to marry him, and I said yes. I thought that I loved him. He was attentive, funny and fun to be around. I think he really did love me, in his own way.

He got orders to go to Guam, and so I had to make the final decision whether or not to really marry this guy. I said a final "yes", so we asked permission from our commanding officer, and he gave the go ahead. One factor was that when two airmen are married, they have to file for joint status to a base and hope there will be a spot for the spouse. If not, the spouse is separated to another base that does have a slot. We were supposed to be married before filing, so that was the plan. The day of our nuptials, I got my orders to Guam. The Commanding

Officer (CO) had pulled some strings and as a wedding present, he got my assignment to Guam to be with Tim. I was so close to putting off the wedding and just waiting till we got to Guam to give us some more time together. After all, five weeks was really quick. That didn't happen and we were married in a military service with a couple of friends as best man and maid of honor. As it turns out, Doug Kross, our best man, wound up in Houston after his service, and we reconnected and stay in touch to this day.

Tim spent his 30 days leave with me in Texas before reporting to his duty station in Guam. We went to Houston so the family could meet Tim. They threw us a party and everyone got along great. After he left, I had to meet his parents on my own, but I fell in love with them immediately. They were great. They lived at Scott AFB, IL, so it was really nice to see another part of the country. I stayed a few days before going home to Houston for some time off. I missed Tim terribly.

While in Houston, the family was really supportive. I had sold my Volkswagen because at the time that I went into the Air Force, the military was not shipping cars overseas for airmen. By the time I left, things had changed, but oh well. I had so many gifts from the family in addition to my own belongings that I wanted to have with me, so I took two duffle bags, two huge suitcases and a box. When I checked into the airport, they told me that I was way over the limit, but since they were going to charge me on the other end before heading overseas, they didn't charge me in Houston. When I checked in four hours early in San Francisco, there was only one person available to check me in, and he didn't charge me anything. Thank goodness because I understand it would have been a lot.

Guam

I flew in a 747 to Hawaii then on to Guam. I fell asleep and could stretch out on the whole row of seats since there were not too many on the plane. I woke up after landing in Hawaii, thinking that I had missed my destination. They were cleaning up the plane and refueling. I can honestly say that I have been to Hawaii, but I never saw any of it, except from the air. Twelve hours to Guam from the U.S. was a long time.

When I arrived in Guam, it was like a comedy unfolding as I shuffled my loot down the line waiting for customs to inspect it all. Tim was on the other end itching to see me, finally, they gave in and let him help me with the luggage. While unloading my stuff for the inspection, there were wrapped presents and other stuff that I had hoped to surprise Tim with, but he got his surprises as they shuffled through everything. After the second suitcase, they gave up and let us through.

As we were leaving the airport, it was like a picture postcard. Everything was so lush and green. The blue water that surrounded the island was as I have never seen blue water before. Coming from Houston, our water in the Gulf of Mexico just didn't look right after this. Palm trees everywhere and it didn't take any time at all before we were at our little hideaway in the boonies. I do mean little. It was a trailer home divided into two apartments. We got the shaft. No drawers in the teeny tiny kitchen. You could almost hold outstretched hands and touch the walls of either side of the place. It was ours, and we were finally together again.

I had never seen a gecko before and they were everywhere, in all sizes and shades of yellow and brown. There was one in the kitchen that would perch himself on the windowsill every night when I did the dishes. He became Henry. I would talk with him as I did the dishes or cooked every night.

This was our beginning, and my first duty station. Tim took me to the base to check in the following day. He was a military dependent and was used to the protocol; he became my sponsor in order to get me acquainted with everything military. Even the base was cool. As we entered the main entrance, there were B52s lined up on the flight line. Just after the entrance, there was a static display of the first B52 to take off from Guam to Vietnam. This was a SAC base which meant Strategic Air Command. This base housed B52s and KC135 tankers. We were the support for the mission.

When you go to any new base, there is an in-briefing. This is where you learn all the dos and don'ts for the area, like 'don't go into the boonies because there are still unexploded armaments from the past'. The culture, regulations, and other beneficial information to stay out of trouble were all discussed.

We were both assigned to the 43rd Civil Engineering Squadron. I was in the plumbing shop and Tim was in the SMART shop. This was the Structural Maintenance and Repair Team. They had a couple of tile layers, carpenters, painters, plumbers and electricians; they went around to the barracks and other buildings and completed all the non-emergency repairs that had been building up over time.

I had a military foreman NCOIC (non-commissioned officer in charge), and a civilian foreman. Master Sergeant Morris and Halomtano were in charge. I liked them both. Sgt. Morris told me that I was not to expect any special attention because I was a woman. There was another woman in the shop, and I didn't expect any special treatment anyway. I was lucky to get a hold of an aluminum 48" pipe wrench. After all, I was only 110 pounds and needed a little help with the huge stuff.

I later found out why Tim and I were not in the same shop. As it turns out, they had my incoming name as Hynes and not Burrows. Halomtano had high blood pressure, and Tim just rubbed him the wrong way, causing his blood pressure to go up. They took advantage of the situation when they found out that we were married, and they moved him to the SMART shop. He resented this, and add to that I was higher ranked than him; we had problems.

After being there for a bit, I took a day off to go and explore the shops on the island. There were shops behind shops and in out-of-the-way places. They were fun to explore. I found a couple of treasures like a cigarette holder made from teakwood, that was a little house. You put the cigarettes in and a bird tipped over and grabbed a cigarette. I got one for my dad, Irvin, and one for Tim. I thought it was cute. I also found a really cool shop that had ivory, jade, and cork art. I got a little education on the subject of jade and ivory: Don't ever clean off the brown stuff on ivory because it shows how old it is, and jade comes in many different shades of green. I found a nice chess set made of ivory that I thought Tim would like since he liked to play. I got it down to $125 with $25 down to purchase for Christmas. There were other cool places to explore on the island, but that would be for another day with Tim.

When I got home and showed him the cigarette holder, he thought it was stupid and just being a jerk about it, so I told him that I would just give it to someone else. He played with it all evening. I had made up my mind that I would not go out of my way to get him anything special again.

One day we were out exploring, and I took him to the ivory store and showed him the chess set to get his opinion on it. He thought it was nothing and started being a jerk again, so I asked the owner for my money back. Later that night, I told him that the chess set was going to be a present for him, and since he had been such a jerk, I canceled the order. What did I get myself into? Soon, he was arguing about everything. There wasn't a day gone by that he wasn't unhappy about something. I didn't dare talk about my day of replacing fire hydrants or re-piping waterlines.

My first week on the job, my partner and I had to repair a toilet; the pipe burst and flooded the house. What a mess. At least the floor was linoleum, and we just had to squeegee it out.

Soon, I started working on the Flush Truck. This was a sewer maintenance truck. It was a two and a half-ton truck that we filled with water at a hydrant and jetted out the sewers on the base. Sgt. Dean Elliott was my partner on the truck. On the back of the truck is the saying, "In our business, flush beats a full house". I always thought that was cute. I worked on replacing PVC pipe going to the beach from the base, and that was tough because this part of the island was made of coral. So, it was always getting punctured. We had to dig with pick axes. What a pain. I got all sorts of experience working there, and it bothered me that I couldn't talk about my exciting day with my husband. He got jealous of my work and anyone I talked to.

I had some fun working with the flush truck. We had to fill it with water from the fire hydrant, for flushing the lines. When we emptied it, we would run over to the abandoned air strip, and I would practice backing it up and parallel parking. While there, we would seek out monitor lizards. These lizards were about four to eight feet long and fast. We would race with them down the old runway while water was running out the bottom drain of the truck. I felt empowered.

At one point in time, I decided to see if I could cross train into something else. I figured if I wasn't in the same field as Tim, maybe things would be better. The Air Force told me that the only way to do that was if there was a medical reason. I told them that I had never lifted the required 35 pounds in basic training, and I was having stomach problems. I actually believe the stomach problems were from all the stress I was under with Tim being a jerk. Anyway, I had to do something to get out of plumbing, so I could get out of the same chain of command as Tim. It just caused too many problems. Well because I was pregnant, they couldn't send me back to the states for training. By this time, I was about six months along, so they found a job available on base at the clinic. I couldn't transfer until after the baby was born, but that was fine with me.

I had been on birth control pills since I was thirteen and wanted to try to regulate myself. The Air

Force takes you off after five years anyway, so I tried and it didn't work. I got pregnant, but before I knew it, I lost it. I was distraught about losing it, so we decided that if I did get pregnant again, it was alright, and things were pretty good between us at the time. Guess what, I did get pregnant again. The pregnancy was going along alright, but I had to leave the plumbing shop; they put me as dispatch and comptroller over six shops. I liked this job.

At one time, during an exercise, I was working the desk and I had to go to a doctor's appointment. My NCOIC told me to call Tim up from the shop to take my desk. When I called him, he was playing cards and refused to come up. The sergeant told me to pull rank and order him to come up. I did, and boy, did crap hit the fan when we got home! This was the first of two times I actually had to pull rank on him. He was not a happy camper.

The Air Force personnel liked to bowl so we joined the league. All the shops had their own team so the plumbing shop played the sheet metal shop and so on. I loved to mess with the guys in the sheet metal shop. It seemed that the drunker they got, the better they bowled, so I would hide their beers sometimes. Of course, Tim had to see if that worked for him as well. He just became more of a jerk when he drank. He had not done much drinking before, so he was still getting drunk on one beer. I did enjoy bowling, but when my pregnancy started showing, Tim said I looked ridiculous, so I felt bad and stopped. I should have stood up to him. He made me feel so beaten down most of the time. When I stopped going bowling, he started an affair with a girl from Dallas. I found this out later on.

Tim was not a very good husband, and I guess that was because he hadn't quite grown up yet. Maybe we started having kids too soon. I wanted to go ahead and have my kids while I was young because I didn't want to be like my parents. I wanted to be in my kids' lives and have fun with them and hopefully, my grandkids too.

Once we were settled into our second dwelling, an apartment, I was able to have my personal stuff from home brought to me in Guam. It was nice to have my "stuff". In it was a shoebox of letters and cards from old friends and boyfriends. Oh my gosh. Tim found them before I got home and started going through them. He got so jealous, so I threw them all away. I would have anyway, but darn it, he needed to stop getting so jealous of everyone.

I tried to get Tim to go to counseling, but he refused. So, we went to a preacher at the base chaplain's office. We saw him for a few months on a weekly basis.

He would acknowledge the problems and discuss the solutions, but when we got home, it was as if he never attended the sessions. This went on for some time and before long, he told me that he wasn't going to go anymore and that he didn't have a problem. He told me not to go back and never step foot in church again. I was so distraught that I agreed.

I wish now that I had stood my ground and put God first. Things didn't get any better. Apparently, no matter what I did, I just couldn't make our life happy. I am sure that by putting God first, I would have either been happier, or divorced a lot sooner, which would not have been a bad thing. Without God in our lives, we had no direction, and I just felt lost.

There were several times that Tim caused me to almost lose the baby. I was a nervous wreck from his physical and emotional abuse. Once we were driving on the back road to the base, and Tim was upset about something. He was driving erratically and drove off the road, and I hit my head. I started having contractions, so I went to the hospital. They checked me out, and after a bit, the contractions stopped.

Another time, while in our apartment, I didn't know where he was, but I started having contractions really bad. We had no phone, so I started checking with some of our neighbors. I almost couldn't walk, but I made it to one of our friends, and there he was drinking. He took me to the hospital, yelling all the while that I had to stop interrupting his time with friends, like it was my fault. The doctors told me that I was too stressed, and Tim would have to help me out. He agreed, but only in the doctor's office. At home, nothing changed.

I found out later that Tim had been flirting with the young girls at the pool while I laid asleep upstairs in our apartment; my buddies downstairs didn't like that one bit. One night, Tim stayed out late drinking with some locals by the pool and got drunk. He came home and passed out. I couldn't handle him by myself, being seven months pregnant, so I planned to go get a friend from the next village to help me; I couldn't find the car keys. Well guess what, Tim let them get stolen, and they took the car. The only person he could identify to the village police was a young guy with "Chamorro Power" tattooed on his chest. As it turns out, that was the guy who stole it. It was found two doors down from his cousin's house where he was hiding. The police picked him up, and we got our car back, but one day shortly after that, he came to our apartment and threatened us into dropping the charges. In Guam, the Saipan mafia was present, and one could pay a small amount to have anyone killed and dropped in the boonies. As soon as he left, we went to the base and straight to the military police. They moved us on base that night and were not allowed off base without an escort. The next day under guard, we moved out of the apartment and into base housing. They couldn't move us back to the states because I was seven months pregnant.

While moving our belongings, I went to the office and told them what was going on. On the way back, I stopped off at a friend's place and told her. When I was leaving, this guy cornered me on the sidewalk and threatened me again. The friend called the village police. By the time I got back to our apartment, the police were whizzing by and brought the guy back for me to identify him. The police were "howleys" (white boys), ex-marines I am guessing. They asked him for his ID, which he had none, but he did have a smart mouth. Before I knew it, one of the policemen had his hand around the back side of his neck and had him on the ground. The other policeman told him that it didn't matter when, but if he ever came near us again, he would have his ass in a sling; it didn't matter if it was next week or a year from now.

The guy was later convicted of statutory rape charges, so we never had to go to court on the auto theft.

After moving onto base, I had hoped that things would get better. They didn't, and life was not exactly rosy. When I had Jeremy, I had hoped that life would get a little better since Tim finally had his boy. When we were exploring names, he wanted to name him Tim Nelson Burrows III. I really didn't want that, so we came up with other names and finally settled on Jeremy William Burrows.

Tim was a plumber, but he still hated to deal with the baby's dirty diaper. Once, when I was out, he got the neighbor to come over and change the diaper. Why is it that when moms are home with the kids, it is just watching the kids, and yet when the fathers are watching the kids, it is babysitting? I never understood this thinking.

One night, I started passing clots. I just put Jeremy in the spare room with me and hoped it would stop. It didn't, and I had a problem waking Tim to get me to the hospital. After yelling for about five minutes, he finally came and helped me to the car. They never did find out what the problem was exactly. I later had similar problems, but they never found out why.

When I was sixteen, I purchased a six-string guitar on credit, my first credit obligation. I was teaching myself to play. One night shortly afFter Jeremy was born, I was cutting Tim's hair. I accidentally cut it too short in the back and he went berserk. He grabbed my guitar and started busting it on the ceiling and floor; we had short ceilings.

I got really scared and took Jeremy to leave, but Tim stopped me and took Jeremy out of my arms. I had to get out of there. I just drove around the base and wound up by the golf course just staring out over the cliffs. I contemplated running the car over the cliffs, but caught myself thinking that I just couldn't leave Jeremy with Tim. I couldn't do that to my child. I felt so trapped in a marriage that I couldn't help. It was broken, and I couldn't fix it. I prayed for God to guide me. I was committed to my marriage and wanted to make it work, no matter what. Tim refused to go to counseling at the hospital because he said that it would prevent him from getting a top-secret clearance. The church was different; they don't report the visits in the medical file.

I just didn't know where to turn. I later became friends with some of the military police, and they told me to call them if anything ever happened again; they would take care of Tim. I almost wanted it to happen then. I didn't want him beat up, though, which is what they sounded as though they would do.

After my maternity leave, I reported to the clinic. I started in the records section, and there was a female airman there that I knew, but she didn't know me. This was the girl that Tim had an affair with while I was pregnant when he was supposedly bowling. Of course, he said that nothing ever happened and the closest he got to doing anything was feeling her boobs, and she never knew that he was married.

On one of our training days, she was explaining to me how the records were made up and what all the information meant. I had her pull Jeremy's chart and explain to me what it all meant. There is a block in the bottom corner that lists the name, rank and squadron of the sponsor. When she read Tim's name, I told her that he was my husband and that was our child. She just got up and left the room. From then on, there was definitely a problem with us working together, especially after I was promoted to Senior Airman, which was over her, just a week or two after I got there.

Fortunately, my squadron commander's assistant and his wife went through lamas with us, so I went to him and explained that I could not work with her directly. He was helpful and sympathetic and made me a floater, so I worked all over the hospital. I spent time in each of the different clinics, which was invaluable training. He later made me the liaison between Naval Regional Medical Center (NRMC) and our hospital, so I was going to the NRMC twice a week. I then became in charge of the Medivac and typed up orders for transfers and organized treatment for all of our servicemen on the island. I sent them to either Clark AFB in the Philippines, to Hickam AFB on Hawaii, or to the states to several bases in California or Texas. It depended on what treatment or procedure they needed. I got to work with the airmen that set up the C130 and outfitted it for medical transport. It was a pretty cool assignment. So, I guess I could thank Tim and that girl for having the affair. It sure worked out for me.

While on the island, I made friends with a sergeant in the Tanker Task Force whose name was Dennis Hynes, the same as my maiden name. We sort of adopted each other as cousins and started socializing with his family. He had a wife and daughter. Dennis told me of a program they had that let airmen ride along on refueling missions. He set me up to go on one. It was pretty cool.

While I was on this flight, we were told how everything works, like the boom, when the B52 would come up for refueling. You lie down on the bench, much like a weight bench, and operate this boom that comes out of the tail of the plane with wings on it. You operate it with a joy stick. At the time that you are hooked up to the B52 (Buff), the boom operator has control of both planes. When one moved the boom around, it made the tail fish-tail. Of course, I wanted to try this. The pilots joked with me about it because they could feel it up in the cockpit. I got to sit in the cockpit of the KC135 in the co-pilots seat. When the pilot said "it's all yours", I thought he was joking, but when I pushed in on the yoke, it moved, and I could see that I was actually flying the plane. We took an aerial tour of the Pacific and the island. I actually flew over the Pacific for about 30 minutes. I got some pretty good aerial shots of the island afterwards.

When I got home and told Tim all about it, he was jealous, so I told him to schedule his own trip. He got slides of the Buff coming in for refueling. They were pretty cool.

Armed Forces Day in Guam was awesome. They brought in planes from the Royal Air Force and a C130, C141, C5, Harrier, Hornet and more. At the Naval base, one could explore an aircraft carrier, a submarine, a frigate, or whatever was in port. Of course, there were certain places on each craft that were off limits since they were active.

During the festivities, there was food at the Chamorro hut village, on base. Each Air Force Squadron would adopt a village on the island. They would get together and build a hut that would depict their ancestral village style. Then on Armed Forces Day, they would get together and make a pig or chicken in the island style and sometimes Hawaiian style. It was all good.

One year our Civil Engineering Squadron had a cock fighting ring. We were not allowed to use the blades, so they put boxing gloves on the chickens. They were beautiful birds. I had never seen pretty chickens. It was hot as all of hades and as the day wore on, the owners of the chickens kept egging each other on, wanting to really fight. By the end of the day, two owners finally succumbed and put blades on their chickens. They fought, well, I wouldn't exactly call it a fight. The poor birds were so hot and run down by then that it just took one swipe, and the other was gone. The two owners got really mad and tried to say that it was the other's fault that this happened. The base commander just told them that they were forbidden to put the blades on them and since they did, it was at their own risk. We didn't do a cock fighting ring again.

There was no dairy on the island, so they had to import milk and most other food goods. At one point, while I was pregnant, they stopped shipping milk. They sent in coconut milk, which I hated. I had to add lots of chocolate to be able to drink it. I had to take calcium pills while pregnant, and when Jeremy was born, the nurses had to cut his nails because they were so long; by the time he was six months, he had six teeth. Thank goodness, he still has pretty good teeth to this day.

I didn't get to see the interior of the island. We took trips around the island once in a while, but for the most part, we stayed on the northern end of the island. There were beaches on the base as well as off and we would snorkel and swim in the beautiful blue water. There was a reef around most of the island, so it was easier to snorkel without the waves tossing you around inside the reef. Once, we went to where the subs and naval ships came into port. There was no reef, so we could see a lot further out. When we were under the water, I saw a shark and immediately got out and never went there again. I figured I'd stay inside the reef.

One time after a storm blew through, we went beach combing. I had a bucket with me and found a slew of coral on the beach. It was the kind that you find in stores back home. It was pretty cool. I loaded up, took it home and bleached it out. I took a box that a toilet had been shipped in, which had the spray foam all around. I wrapped the coral the best I could and shipped it back home. Mother told me that it was mostly all broken up. No big pieces.

The native Guamanians were really nice and friendly people and were predominately Catholic. Their customs were very inviting. Once, after we first moved there, we were driving around and came across a stand. We thought it was a commerce operation, and the local people invited us to stay and eat. I thought this was strange, but we did and enjoyed their local cuisine, listening as best we could to what they were saying. I had taken a year of Spanish in high school, so I was able to watch their body language and figure out what they were saying.

The island was like a picture, so I really enjoyed taking a lot of pictures. We could develop the slides ourselves and the Base Exchange sold us what we needed. It was pretty cheap, so we took a bunch. The island had been invaded by several countries such as Spain, Japan and the United States. When Japan invaded, they killed the local men because they were tall and scary looking. Then they would mix with the local women, so the men on the island became shorter than their ancestors.

The island was only eight by thirty-five miles long with its highest elevation being Mount Lamlam, just over 1300 feet. The northern part of the island was mostly coral, and the southern was volcanic with a lush jungle, wild animals, and rats the size of large cats. The waters were so blue with so many sea shells and coral all around. The beaches were coral, so one could not go barefooted, and there were also poisonous sea critters so one normally wore water shoes in the water as well. They had fiestas several times a year where they would invite the squadron that adopted them, and a good time was had by all. Plenty of drinking and eating was always going on; no one left hungry. The temperature ranged from 70 to 102 degrees, and there was a rainy season where it rained somewhere on the island every day. It may not have been much of a shower, but it sure kept everything green. During the typhoon season, everyone got a bit tense, and of course, there was the coconut patrol. I had to do it one time. We just go around the base picking up all the coconuts lying about, so they wouldn't become projectiles.

When we first moved to Guam, I wanted to make Tim a German chocolate cake, so I went to the store to try to find shredded coconut. Someone made the realization that I must have just moved there. They said, "Just go out into the yard and pick up a coconut." I didn't know that those big green or brown pods were coconuts. I was thinking of the small round coconut I saw in the grocery stores. I was the dumb Howley this time.

One of the major squadrons on the base was the B52 Alert Birds. The pilots would stay in special barracks during their assignment period. There was a special route from their barracks to the flight line for them. When the sirens went off, the traffic was stopped next to this route, so the pilots could get to their planes in record time. I remember this happening several times. I would often think of these men heading off to parts unknown. During some of the exercises, they would have to be airborne for a period of time with the nukes. This was our main mission on the base, to support these pilots.

Off and on, Tim and I got along great; everything would be going so smoothly, then out of the dark came another explosion. I would never know what would set him off. I couldn't tell if he was bipolar or what. He just wouldn't recognize that he had a problem. He spent money left and right, and we barely made ends meet. He would barter and trade stuff without discussing it with me. I tried to never call him bad names, but one time I did call him a "son of a bitch". He threw me across the room. I landed on the chase that went out onto the floor, but my head hit the floor on the other side and was I knocked out. I came to consciousness in his arms. He told me that I should never make him mad, and that it was my fault I got knocked out.

When I was pregnant with Jeremy, my commander gave us a 75-gallon aquarium. I had taken oceanography in high school and knew how to set up a salt water aquarium. We would fight over how much gravel to put on top of the underground filter grate. I finally gave up and let him contaminate the tank with too much, which he did. We had gone out to the ocean and collected all sorts of fish, conk shells, star fish of different sorts, and even got an eel. It was a small eel, but I think it killed the small turkey fish we had. We had no top on the tank, and one day I came home from work and found one of the star fish half-hanging out of the tank. We eventually had to let everything go back into the ocean, what survived anyway. Tim just wouldn't listen to me, and the tank got all black. It was pretty cool though, at least until that point.

When we got orders for our next assignment, it was to Wyoming. I have to admit that I didn't know where Guam was when we first got our assignment, and now I felt really stupid because I wasn't sure which side of the US Wyoming was on. We were moving from where it never gets colder than 70 to where it never gets warmer than 70. A month prior to leaving, we readied our car to be shipped to San Francisco.

After clearing out of base housing, we moved into a hotel for a few days. What do you know? A typhoon hits the island. It was pretty cool to see the water from the pool being blown out of it, and the palm trees bending almost all the way to the ground. We survived the typhoon, and soon after, left the island.

We took a 747 back to the good ole USA. Jeremy was only ten months old and still in diapers. When we arrived in Hawaii, the customs went through everything, including Jeremy's diaper. I asked them if they wanted to see the one I just tossed into the trash. They didn't have much of a sense of humor. We didn't get to see anything of Hawaii, but we were on our way and couldn't wait to touch down in San Francisco. We left Guam at around 8 p.m. and arrived in California at 7 p.m. the same day. Jet lag was a major factor. We checked into our hotel, but couldn't sleep, so we just went and got our car and took off. We were in LA by 3 a.m. The southern route to Texas is one of the most boring routes in the US. I couldn't talk Tim into doing any site-seeing, like the Grand Canyon, so on to Texas we went. We did stop at Davis Monthon AFB for the night, and it just so happened that they were showing the "Who shot JR" episode of "Dallas". In Guam, we got all the shows a week later than stateside, so it was cool that we were able to see this episode. Small pleasures didn't come too often.

I took videos of our trip, but looking at them later, we couldn't tell which state we were in because it was all just desert and sage brush.

When we hit El Paso, Texas, it was about two in the morning, and I was driving. When you are in the service, your driver's license does not expire, and I kept mine in a two-pocket case with my military ID. When the customs guard stopped us at the station, he asked if we had any non-Americans in the car. I was tired and stupid and told him we had a gook in the back. He looked at my driver's license and asked why my license had expired and where were we coming from. I told him we were military and coming from Guam. He asked where that was. I answered, "Go west to San Francisco and keep going." He looked at our license plate and asked what "Hafa Adai" was. I told him that it was a common expression in Guam that meant "hello" or "have a good day". He just laughed and said, "It must have been a long night." I said, "Yep, it sure has," and we drove on.

We made it to Houston and stayed with my mother in her apartment. We could not go out until Jeremy was good and asleep. I didn't realize that Mother had a phobia about little kids. I guess having seven children and not being able to manage such a large family by herself, she just couldn't cope with little kids anymore.

We visited with all the family in Houston, and really enjoyed being home. We flew to Florida to see the in-laws and met Tim's grandparents and great-grandmother. We got a four-generation picture, which was pretty cool. It was nice seeing Tim Sr. and Angie again as well. I loved the grandparents. They were good ole down home folks. We stayed a few days, then flew back to Houston where we picked up our car and drove to Illinois.

The in-laws were stationed at Scott AFB in Illinois and it was winter, so we got to play in the snow. This was the first time for Jeremy and me to actually play in this much snow. I had fun. We celebrated Jeremy's first birthday there and had a pretty good time. After a few days, we left Jeremy with the in-laws and drove to Wyoming.

Wyoming

It was a nice trip. We didn't fight much at all the whole trip, as I can remember. Maybe I'm just being optimistic. We checked into the base, F.E. Warren AFB in Cheyenne. I was in the medical squadron and Tim in plumbing still. The base used to be an Army Fort called Fort Russell. It is the oldest continuously active military installation within the Air Force. It was home to the 90th Missile Wing which became the nation's first operational Minuteman ICBM base with the introduction of the Atlas missile in 1958. Of course, all the missiles were not confined just to the Cheyenne vicinity, but spread out over several states; all were under control of F.E. Warren AFB. I never went to any of the silos, but Tim did. It was pretty cool to see the missile carriers bring the missile in for repair. The truck would pull up to the hole in the ground and lift the full payload straight up, and the missile would be lowered into the hole. They would essentially work on them underground. We also housed a helicopter squadron for escorting the missiles to and from the silos. They would also help with search and rescue sometimes.

The officers' housing on the base were the old red brick homes that looked pretty cool when there was a blanket of snow on the ground all around them. My first day to drive a military truck in the snow was scary. I spun around on the ice, so I learned really quickly not to put the brakes on too fast while driving on ice.

We found a bi-level house off base on the other side of town within our financial range and moved in right away. Our goods arrived quickly after getting the house, so we were able to get things organized before Jeremy came home. I sure missed him.

When we got to our duty station, I had to set up checking accounts. It was not like it is today when you can bank anywhere and just move money around. Our military pay stopped for a while until we got it set up at the bank. I had decided to get separate accounts so that

Tim could see just who was spending all the money. He didn't like it too much, but that was the only way I was going to do it. We would split the bills and whatever was left over, each of us had to decide to save or spend it.

Just before Christmas, the in-laws brought Jeremy to us. I was so glad to have him back in my arms again. They spent a few days with us, then went back to Illinois. The arguing started again, and it didn't matter what I said or did, Tim would always find something to gripe about. After only a few weeks there, I decided to take a Saturday and go the mall in Ft. Collins, CO with a woman I worked with. I had told her a little about what had been going on with Tim. I needed someone to confide in. We had started seeing the base psychologist, and Tim would agree to things in the session, but then ignore it when we got home. I just needed to get away for the day, and Tim was on call, so he couldn't go; thank goodness.

Before I left, Tim said that he didn't have any money and needed some so he could eat on base. I told him that it was too bad and I would not give him any. He could eat at home. When my friend came to pick me up, I took Jeremy out to the car and strapped him in. I remembered that Tim was a signer on my account, so I went back into the house to get my checks, so he couldn't clean me out. He grabbed me and started throwing me around and onto the couch and bouncing on me.

At one point, he threw me up against the window, and my friend saw what was happening. She got the deputy from across the street. As soon as he came in, I bolted out the door. I didn't get to the mall that day; instead I went to my First Sergeant and told him what had happened. He got Tim's First Sergeant to call him in on a fake call, so I could go get some stuff from the house. I moved in with my friend about three miles away and went to see the psychologist. When I told him what had happened, he ordered us both to stay away from each other. After a few days, my commander called me and told me to please call Tim's parents because Tim was calling him at all hours of the night. I called them and told them what was going on and that I couldn't live like that anymore. I was no longer trapped on an island and needed some space for a bit. They were very understanding. A few days later, I was at work, and one of the nurses came to me to say that Tim had been admitted for dehydration and was asking for me. I went to him and told him that I couldn't live this way anymore and he needed to change. He promised to stop smoking and hitting me. I said that I would move back home.

During this two-week separation, I met with a man, a couple of times, who helped me to see that I didn't have to be treated like a punching bag. He was very kind and lent a listening ear. That was all it was, but I guess I needed that; ok, we kissed too. I still loved Tim and just wanted to have a normal life with him, but what did I know about normal?

I moved back into the house and Tim was discharged a few days later. The Captain that ordered us to stay apart was furious. He said that he had "ordered" us to stay away from each other and that order was to be upheld. I almost got a formal reprimand. I told him that I didn't feel that it was up to him to order a married couple to stay apart when they finally work things out. I think he was just on a power trip. He never explained any details about upholding the order or punishment, so oh well.

Tim came home and didn't stop smoking, but he did stop hitting me. It seemed to be alright for a little while, and then the verbal abuse started again. For the most part we got along, so we started talking about having another baby. I wanted to wait a bit longer, so three months after we got back together, we started trying, and I got pregnant. I think it was more fun not knowing what sex the baby was. Nowadays everyone wants to know what it is so they can plan. Well not knowing was half the fun of it.

After just a few months of pregnancy, we were accepted to base housing. I didn't really get to know any of the neighbors in the other neighborhood because I was ashamed of myself and Tim. While in Guam, some of our friends stopped coming around because they hated the way he treated me. I lost too many friends because of him; to be honest, it was also because I was afraid to take up for myself and be more assertive.

First, we moved onto base into a single house. It was a two-bedroom house and not quite as nice as our house off base, but it was cheaper. The military gives you a housing allowance if you are married and live off base. When we moved on base, of course, they take that back. That was alright with me. We had less of a commute.

I made a couple of visits back home to Houston and on one of my visits, Gene and I were able to talk and get a lot of things straightened out. He set me straight by telling me that he didn't realize how he had made me feel all those years ago. Since we didn't talk very much over the years, I had been storing up all this depression, thinking that my brother didn't care at all. Now we were great.

Winter soon set in. The winters were brutal, and the wind never stopped, or so it seemed. Once when I took Jeremy to the babysitter, he was dressed in his snow suit, and the wind blew him off the stoop, which was elevated about a foot or so. The snow looked so cool on the base. F.E. Warren AFB was like something out of the Old West with the red brick buildings and a solid blanket of snow all around. Sometimes I would stop the car and jump out and run through the snow. I liked to be the first to make tracks. I loved the sound of the crunch of snow under my boots. There were icicles hanging from the bare branches, and it looked like life just stood still. Sometimes Tim would get into his moods and start saying stupid stuff like "I don't want this baby" and "I didn't agree to this in the first place". I think he did this sometimes just to cause an argument.

While in the service, if you are underweight or overweight, you could get kicked out unless you were under a doctor's care. I was 104 pounds before I got pregnant, and the doctors told me that there was just no more they could do for me. They had tried the hypoglycemic diet, diabetic diet and just plain eating too much. None of this worked; I just couldn't get my weight up to the 111 pounds required. So, when I got pregnant, I decided to get out because they were going to kick me out anyway, and Tim preferred I get out and take care of the kids. I think he just wanted me to get out so he could outrank me. I scheduled my discharge for the day after I made Sergeant, which was November 2, 1981. I was really hoping that this would make Tim happy, and then we would be happier.

I was able to stay at home with Jeremy and be a mom. I loved that aspect of it. Things were pretty good with Tim and I as well. There were some bumps, of course, and I started to think that he just didn't know any other way. He was jealous all the time, which caused problems. It didn't matter what I said or did; he would think that I was fooling around on him.

In January, Anne was born. There were blizzard conditions, and we had to get to the hospital after dropping Jeremy off at a friend's house down the street. We made it to the base hospital that evening, and she was born the next morning. So now I could say that both my kids were born in winter, one in scorching temperatures and the other in a blizzard.

Not too much longer after Anne was born, we moved into a bigger house with three bedrooms. It was in a courtyard with a U shape and two duplexes. We became friends with Jake and Val from across the street. They were a little older than us, but we got along great and played pinochle every week. The other people in our courtyard were alright too. We were actually socializing with most of them on a regular basis. After a while, I really did get tired of all the cussing around my kids. They would think it was funny when their kids would repeat what they had said. I didn't.

In February of 1983, my grandmother died, and Betsy called me to tell me about it and that she would pay for me to come down to Texas for the services. So, the kids and I went to Houston. Tim was mad because he didn't get to go, but I told him that I needed some time to think anyway.

While I was in Houston, seeing all the family and a few old friends, I decided that I didn't deserve to be treated the way Tim was treating me. I never told the family just how bad it was. When I returned from Houston, Tim and I sat down and talked. While we were talking, he wanted Jeremy to come to him, but the way

Tim said it scared Jeremy, so he just snuggled up next to me for protection. When this happened, Tim got mad and started to slap him. When I put up my hand to stop him, I nicked his face and he started in on me. That was it. I just couldn't continue living like that; nobody lays a hand on my kid. We needed to try a trial separation. He would have no part of it. I told him to put in for a remote assignment. Then, I came up with a really stupid idea that I didn't actually think he would go for, to just live together but in separate rooms. We'd live our lives separately as roommates, and as long as the kids were taken care of, we'd see whomever we want. He went for it. How dumb can you get? But OK. We tried this for a while.

The following month, my only uncle on my mother's side died. He'd been diagnosed with cancer, and the doctors gave him six months to live. He tried different experimental treatments at MD Anderson, and he lived for six years. Finally, he had enough and stopped all the treatments. He left behind six girls and a wife.

I was working at the NCO club as a cocktail waitress and bar-back. Tips were usually pretty good, so I was able to save up a little bit of money. One of the guys that would come in all the time became friends with me, and we got closer. He was a photographer with the base photo lab, so we had something in common. I would go to his place once in a while and he taught me that sex can be a lot more fun and respectful than I had known with Tim. I tried to get Tim to give me a divorce, and he just wouldn't go for it. He told me that he would fight me for the kids. Then, when that didn't faze me, he wanted to split up the kids. He would take Jeremy, and Anne would go with me, and never the two would meet. I told him that he was deranged for even suggesting that, knowing how I lived my childhood. He put in for a remote assignment, but didn't know how long it would take. I figured he was seeing someone, but didn't really want to know who, so I didn't press it. I really didn't care.

One night I told Tim I had to get to work, and he needed to stay home and take care of the kids. I left and actually went to Rob's place. When I returned to the NCO club for my shift, my boss called me in and told me that Tim had come in looking for me. I went home and Val was there watching the kids. She told me that Jake had taken Tim to the emergency room, he had flipped out. I went to the emergency room, and Jake stopped me right away calling me a slut. Tim came to me and asked me where I was, and was I with someone? I hesitated and thought for a brief moment; this was my chance to maybe get the divorce I'd been wanting. I said yes and left.

When I got off work around two in the morning, he was waiting for me in the living room. He was calmer than I had seen him in a long time. He told me to go pack, and he had called the Military Police to escort my fanny off base without the kids. I told him he was crazy, that I was not leaving without the kids. The MPs came and told him that I had the right to stay there; they called his First Sergeant, and he came over. Tim went to stay in the barracks, and we filed for divorce the next day. I went to the welfare department to see what they could help me with to get me back on my feet. I found an apartment, and they paid the deposit and three month's rent. I got $98 in food stamps, I was already on WIC, and they paid for a sitter after I found a job working for Domino's.

While we were packing our stuff, Tim was being good. He kept trying to get me to stop the divorce. He wanted me back and even bought me a ring from the Base Exchange. It was a cheap thing, only $14, but I knew he didn't have any money to spare. I told him that maybe we could become friends and maybe eventually date again. Who knows where life takes us? I told him to hang onto the ring and maybe if we could get beyond all this, we would see. I wasn't completely discounting the chance to get back together; he could give it back to me then. I had given up plumbing, the Air Force, and now there was nothing left for me to give up that would make him happy. I guess I was pretty stupid to even think of wanting to get back with him. I was hoping that maybe, on his own, he would grow up.

A few weeks later, I was at a party with some friends. They were talking about the ring that Tim had given to an old neighbor of ours. Supposedly he had given her my ring and asked her to marry him after her husband returned their daughter and got a divorce. Her husband had kidnapped their daughter and took off. I guess I saw that as a final goodbye to any possibility of getting back with Tim, and besides that was my ring first. The green-eyed monster came out. I called Tim and told him my feelings. He came over that night and we made love one last time. He got my ring back from the other woman, and we decided that it just wasn't going to work with us.

There is only a twenty-day waiting period for the divorce to become final. I agreed to pay the lawyer and Tim kept calling him and running up the bill. He even accused me of sleeping with the lawyer. It got to the point that I couldn't wait until the divorce was final.

I started going back to church. I joined the Methodist Church in Cheyenne. The class I was in was pretty interesting. The instructor was a history professor, and most everyone in class was someone in the government. We would take a topic out of the newspaper and discuss how they would have handled it in biblical days.

I got involved with the youth. There was such a large group of children that they needed all the help they could get. I had a great time. Tim would take the kids sometimes when I was at MYF meetings and they had a daycare available for us at other times. One of our trips with the youth was to Estes Park in Colorado. We went to a YMCA camp in the Rockies. It was so beautiful with snow everywhere. I learned to cross-country ski and decided I really didn't like it. It was so nice to get away from everything. We did devotionals at night and were able to just take some time to ourselves for reflection. I felt closer to God in the stillness of the forest and the beauty of the snow-covered mountains. I felt that my life was finally getting back on track. I really started to notice that with my old friend, Jesus, back in my life, I felt more in control.

While working at Domino's, I had several adventures. Within the first week, I got caught in a snow bank and got a ticket for running a stop sign (my car would die if I let it idle, so I did a rolling stop). I asked Tim to help pull me out of the snow bank, but he refused. I got my neighbor at the apartments to help me. He took pity on me and would get up for work and charge the battery for me almost every day. He was such a great guy. He was an older man, and I would fix him dinner once in a while as a thank you.

I did have fun working at Domino's, especially when I got to make the pizzas. I learned to fly the dough, and we used the real pizza ovens, not the conveyer ovens they use now.

I worked nights, so it was hard to find a sitter that would watch the kids at night. I did find an older couple, maybe in their late 50s or early 60s. They were also watching an infant of someone prominent, so I felt pretty good about it, and they were on the approved list from welfare.

Tim kept trying to get the kids for an evening during the week, which made it hard when I had a sitter who needed the five days. He just wouldn't accept the regular schedule of every other weekend.

One night I had off, I went to Jake and Val's house for a visit. I noticed Tim's truck next door at one of our other neighbor's house. She was the one whose husband had taken off with their daughter. I went over there to see if he wanted to take the kids that weekend. He didn't want to take them camping with his girlfriend. I just didn't understand why he didn't want to spend time with the kids. We would be leaving for Houston soon, and he might never see them again. We got into an argument, and I left. When I got back home around 10:30, the MPs called and said that I had to come back up to the base and answer charges of disturbing the peace. I asked them if I could come up the next day since I had just gotten the kids down for the night. They told me that if I didn't come up right away, they would send the civilian police and probably put me in jail.

I went and filled out a report. I saw Tim there filling out some paperwork. I couldn't believe that he would do this after all the arguing we had done in the past. He told me that it was his girlfriend making him do it. Like I believed that. I finished my paperwork and left. Nothing came of it.

I started dating my manager, Jerry, and convinced him to let me work days, so that it would be easier for daycare. One day I picked up the kids and went home. I was exhausted and just fed the kids pizza at their little table. When they finished, I was cleaning them up and noticed make-up coming off of Anne's face, covering up a huge bruise. It was in the shape of a hand. I freaked out. I called the sitter and only got their daughter. Jeremy had told me that the man had slapped her because she wouldn't pick up her toys. I called Tim and told him what had happened and to meet me at the hospital emergency room. He was too busy for such things, but came anyway. The doctor took x-rays and checked her out. The MPs were called and they told me that there was nothing they could do since it happened off base; I would need to go to the civilian police. So, we went and they took pictures every day for several days. I immediately went to the welfare department and reported them. They would lose their license immediately.

I had to go see a judge. As soon as I told him who it was that had done this, he got on the phone to call his wife and told her to go pick up their child. He turned to me and said that it was a conflict of interest for him to take the case because they were also watching his baby. I asked him what could be done. He told me that all they would get would be a slap on the wrist, license revoked, and maybe a $100 fine. I would have to fly back for the trial. I was getting ready to move back to Texas, so I left and found another sitter. The bruises went away, but I felt horrible about what happened to my child.

About this time, I was beginning to wonder why God was letting all these things happen to my family. I would cry myself to sleep. I felt as though my friend, Jesus, had left me all alone. My praying went on into the night, and between the crying and praying, I didn't get much sleep some nights. I just wasn't ready to raise these kids on my own. After a few sleepless nights, I finally reached deep down inside and found the strength to go on. I remembered that God doesn't leave us alone.

One time, while at my apartment, blood clots started flowing like water out of me. I didn't know what to do. I became pretty weak and managed to get Jerry, who was visiting another neighbor, to take me to the VA. They admitted me, but didn't know what to do. They were not equipped yet for women coming out of the service. They cleared out a small room that had four beds, so I could have privacy. I was to stay in bed, and hopefully, they could find out why I was bleeding so badly. Tim was called in from one of the missile silos to take care of the kids. He came to see me once and started bullying me. The guys across the hall came and asked if they could help me. They were a little protective of me, maybe because I was the only woman in the hospital. Tim got mad and asked why didn't my boyfriend watch the kids and why did he have to come in to take care of them? Well, duh, they were his kids and not Jerry's responsibility. The doctors never did find out why I had been bleeding clots so bad, but it did stop and I went home. The doctor thought that maybe I had a spontaneous abortion, and he told Jerry that. He was upset and I told both him and the doctor that was an impossibility because I had my tubes tied.

Tim got assigned to Korea. The remote assignment finally came in, but too late. I found out that he could have our goods shipped anywhere because the kids were his dependents. He refused to sign the papers. It cost him nothing, but he wanted to be vindictive. I finally had to threaten him to sign since he was a month behind on the child support. He finally signed the papers, and we were able to move everything to Houston.

I got the apartment settled, did a tune up on my car and said my goodbyes to everyone. The radiator and the oil pan had a leak, so I loaded up on water and oil. I stayed on base at Jake and Val's house for the night before taking off for Houston. While I was trying to get everything finished up, I asked Tim if he would please spend the day with the kids since he wouldn't be seeing them again for a long time. He complained that he had to finish packing his room in the barracks and couldn't take the kids. He had known about his move for two weeks, and as usual, he waited till the last minute. He did finally take them and spend a few hours with them.

While at Jake and Val's house, Jake told me why he had been so rough on me that night at the emergency room. With his first wife, he had come home early and caught her in bed with another man. I told him that it wasn't like that with Tim and me. I explained everything. I told him that Tim had come home one night after drinking heavy at their house and accused me of letting a guy put his hand under my skirt at one of Jake's parties. He proceeded to yell and slap me around. Jake said that he and another guy wanted to see what it would take to get him riled up so they were giving him white lightning while they were drinking water. They were egging him on by telling him all sorts of lies about me. He said that Tim never got riled. He felt awful when I told him what happened at home that night. We cleared the air on everything and were good friends again.

Before leaving, I called my mother and asked her to loan me $300 until I got back to Houston. I only had about $500 on me; with a leaky car, I just wanted a little cushion. She refused and told me that she had come all the way to Houston with all of us and almost no money, and I could do the same. She told me that I shouldn't ask any of my siblings either. I called Mom Deardan, and she sent it to me the next day.

Back to Texas

This trip would be my first long trip by myself. The kids traveled pretty well. Anne was one and Jeremy was three years old. Every time I stopped, I had to put water and oil in the car. I had made arrangements with a close friend to let me stay at his sister's house in San Angelo, so that took care of one night. I paid to stay in a campground in the car another night, and then on to Houston. We arrived on the 9th of September, I believe. When I got to the Deardans house in Bellville, TX, I paid them back the $300 and spent the night. The next morning, we were off to Houston.

Not long after arriving at Betsy's house, she got a call from the YMCA in downtown Houston saying that they had found our brother's body in his room. Now we had to plan another funeral. I didn't even know he was in Houston. With my grandmother, Munnie, dying, then my Uncle Mat, now my brother, and not to mention my divorce earlier in the year, that year was a bad one.

I settled in with Annette and her boyfriend with my kids. She lived in a two-story townhouse. We made it work. I went on interviews and tried to get a job as a plumber, but no one wanted to hire me because I didn't have a certificate as a plumber's helper, and they weren't too interested in helping me get it. Men just didn't want a woman in that type of work. I finally got a job with a home health care company next door to Betsy's work. I moved in with Mother for a little while.

After a month, I had a job and moved into a duplex not far from work. I got the kids into daycare and I was finally back on my feet, or at least close to it. I didn't make much, but with the $300 a month child support and my salary, I did make ends meet. Finances were pretty tight though. The house was actually part of a duplex where they had divided an old house, and I got jipped with no kitchen. Thank goodness, I had a microwave and a cooler. A friend of mine found a refrigerator on the side of the freeway. He said he had to replace a motor mount, and other than that, it was a new appliance. The family got me a gas range for Christmas and I was set.

I liked my job, but the administrator was a flake. Richard, Charles, and Wesley were all gay, and I really didn't care, but Richard was for sure flaming. He should have left it out of the office. Charles Beers owned the business, and Wesley was the part time bookkeeper. I was the admin assistant. I did the coding for all the patients' billing and ran down providers for the provider services. I wrote the doctor's orders and had to track them down to get their signatures. Dealing with Medicare, Medicaid and other insurance companies was interesting, but dealing with Richard was my biggest challenge. Before long, Charles wanted me to take over running the company, so I finally got a raise. The salary was not what it should have been, and Charles' parents had the final say. With the company not making much money, I never got any more money.

The office was in Charles' garage apartment, which was not very big. We started getting more clients and needed more room for more staff, so we moved into the house and Charles moved into the apartment. Within a year's time, I brought the company up from just six medical patients to twenty and fourteen provider clients to one hundred eleven. I still didn't get a raise.

While in Wyoming, I had a friend named Aaron. He was a friend to both Tim and me. After I got divorced, Aaron and I became pretty close, and he asked me to marry him. He was heading to Washington on assignment, and I was heading to Houston, so we figured that we would see what time would bring. We stayed in touch and maybe he was the lifeline I needed for a while. I had said yes, and even though I didn't have a phone, we wrote often. We figured that when he got out in two years, he would move down to Houston with me. It was going to be a long engagement. I thought that I really did love him, but I think I was more in love with the idea. Aaron loved the kids and me, and he was sort of a link to another part of my life that I just couldn't discount yet.

In November, I was driving around and went over to Dwayne's house where there was a man working on his car. I asked him if he knew of Dwayne. He told me that he was working in Midland, and his mom still owned the house. I gave him my card and asked him to tell Dwayne to call me, and if he lost the card, just tell him that the crazy red head was back in town. I figured that he could find me somehow.

Dwayne

Betsy worked next door, so we ate lunch together most days. One Friday in February, she was really quiet and had a grin on her face. By the end of the day, I got a call from Dwayne. He was getting back into town from Midland for the weekend and wanted to get together. I told him that I had two kids now. He said, "I know, this ought to be interesting," We made arrangements for him to come to my house that night. When I was leaving work, Betsy was also. I was so excited. I told her that Dwayne had called. She was so funny; she said that he had called her the night before and got caught up.

Dwayne came over and met the kids. He put Anne on his knee, and she freaked out. She never liked men to pick her up. I guess she was still scared because of how Tim was. She looked at me in terror, and I told her that it was alright. She settled in and won his heart immediately.

Jeremy was my little man. He would soothe me when I was down. He would tell me, "Mommy, I'm here and I'll be nice to you, I won't hurt you like Daddy did." He used to freak out when Dwayne and I would wrestle around. He didn't understand that we were just playing. He was my comfort. I am so glad that they were so young when all this happened, and they don't remember the bad times.

Dwayne knew about Aaron, and I was even dating another old friend, Chuck. Chuck and I dated while we were in high school. Chuck was a really nice guy, but he wasn't my idea of a husband. I know I broke his heart when I told him that I just couldn't establish a closer relationship.

Dwayne was working in Midland, Texas, and had an apartment in Houston. He would come into town every other weekend and spent the weekends with us. He became a constant in our lives, and I had wished that we were closer, but he wasn't "in love" with me, I think. He grew to love the kids and told me that no matter what happened to us, he hoped that he could continue to spend time with my children.

He took us around Houston to parks and had fun with us, no matter what we did. I was falling in love with him again, but this time I knew what it meant to fall in love. I was at a quandary with both Aaron and Dwayne. I didn't really know how I should handle it. I told Aaron of my misgivings, and he decided to come down to Houston and see if we were really meant to be together. I was so mixed up. I knew I loved Aaron and didn't think that Dwayne loved me the way I wanted him to.

It was June, and Dwayne was planning a trip to Wyoming with his buddies to go hiking. He moved back into his apartment, and Aaron came into town. Dwayne told me to give Aaron a chance and try not to contact him. Dwayne had paid for me to have a phone, so I felt a little more connected with the world.

Aaron and I just didn't mesh, so after only three days, I was convinced that I really did love Dwayne and that was who I really wanted to be with. I talked with Charles, my boss, about my predicament. He told me that maybe Dwayne did love me, but he couldn't make that decision for me. I needed to make that decision all on my own. Charles had talked with Dwayne already. I guess I wanted him to be my knight in shining armor and just come and sweep me off my feet. Well, it doesn't work like that. I called Dwayne before he left for Wyoming and went over to his place to see him. We talked...and let's just say that we were both glad I did. He didn't admit that he loved me, but I figured that it would come, or at least I had prayed for it.

I had to do some heavy praying for guidance now. I knew He had a plan, and I hoped that meant that Dwayne and I were supposed to be together. Of course, He never asks us our opinion. I felt that my life was so mixed up, but I knew that no matter what happened, God was there with me.

Aaron left the following weekend, and we parted as friends. Dwayne went up to Wyoming, and after a few days, he called me. He had gotten tired of his time up in the mountains, but couldn't leave because his friends were still up on the mountain.

When they returned, his friends told me that he was acting all weird and figured that was when he decided that he did love me enough to go to the next level of our relationship.

Dwayne liked to go target shooting, so we got Mother to watch the kids, and he took me shooting. I had never shot a hand gun before. I'd only shot a .22 caliber rifle in JROTC and earned expert Marksman. We went to an indoor range, and I did pretty well. He thought I had been lying to him about my having shot a hand gun. I did a grouping of about two inches from 25 feet. All the way home, he kept telling me that I had shot really well, and he just couldn't believe that I had never shot a hand gun. When we got home, Mother asked how I had done. Dwayne said that I did great and better than he had done his first time out. She told him, "It sounds like she hasn't lost her touch." He really didn't believe me.

One of our visits to Betsy and Billy's house, their friend, Anthony, was there. I was talking to him for a few minutes. Dwayne knew that I had dated Anthony. He was quiet all the way home. While I was putting the kids to bed, Dwayne left without telling me.

The following day, Dwayne was supposed to take us to the park, but never showed up. We were all disappointed. His phone had been transferred to mine, so I couldn't call him. He finally showed up, later that night, with no explanation. I didn't know what to say. I guess he was a little jealous of my talking to Anthony.

Once, when we were both paying our bills, he noticed that I had only nine dollars in my account after paying everything. He wanted me to sign the back of a check, but wouldn't let me see what it was for. He finally told me that he wanted me to have a little extra in my account. The next day my grandmother's estate was settled, and Betsy gave me the check from it, which was about $2500; I immediately went to the bank and deposited it. When Dwayne deposited his check for $1500, he was expecting to see a balance of $1509 and was surprised to see it was more. He thought I was hiding something, but I explained to him about the inheritance. We both just laughed.

Not long after that he moved all his money into my account, and we were making plans to move into another apartment together. We had been looking at a set of living room furniture that had entertainment shelving, a matching coffee table, and end tables at a local store that bragged about same day delivery. When we signed the lease for an apartment and were moving in, I went to the furniture store and ordered the set we had been looking at. They delivered the same day, but it was not all brand new. Two pieces of the wall unit were floor models, and had cracked veneer from 100-watt bulbs. I called the company and they insisted that was what I ordered. I told them that was not what I ordered. The salesman was an old school mate of mine and he checked the warehouse while I was there, and they had them all in. I wanted them to replace the two pieces. They refused, so I put a stop payment on the check since they refused to pick them up.

The apartment we were moving into was on the bottom floor, and as we were moving in, there were two families moving in upstairs. The teenagers were spitting on the sidewalk just outside our apartment and bouncing a basketball on our wall. This was very annoying. We went to the apartment office and asked to be moved to another apartment on the second floor. The manager was out, but the person told us that we could move after one opened up the following month. We had paid the deposit and still needed to sign the agreement and pay the first month's rent. We refused to do that until the manager was back in the office and would guarantee our move to another apartment.

On Monday, after moving from two separate households, I came home to our new apartment. I couldn't get into the apartment and thought that Dwayne had given me the wrong key. He finally showed up after work and told me that was the only key. There was no one in the office and we were determined to fix this ourselves. Dwayne and Gordan, his partner, were ready to break into the patio door but found the side window was unlocked. We moved out in two hours. Now mind you, I had unpacked everything the previous weekend as the guys were unloading. This had to be the fastest move in history. We had everything packed back up and loaded and the trucks sitting in the shop in just over two hours.

I got calls from the furniture store threatening to send the check to the district attorney's office. I called the district attorney's office to see what would be done. They told me that they would subpoena the account and verify the funds were in there when the check was written. If the funds were there they would then send the check back to the company. There was nothing more they could do. So with the following call from the company, I told them that they needed to order us the correct furniture.

They said that it was on back order, or they could give us a lower grade set. It's funny because this company now boasts that "there will never be a back-order slip". These calls went on for two weeks. We had moved the furniture, so I had to send a letter by registered mail to show where they could pick up the furniture. I got so tired of the calls that Dwayne went there to talk with someone in the warehouse. She was not too happy and claimed that Dwayne cussed her out. They kept telling me about sending the check to the DA's office, and I told them to go ahead because I knew there was nothing they could do. The money was in the account. One final call from them and I had finally had enough. I asked them if they would sign for the furniture if we brought it back, and they said "no". Would they pick it up? The answer was "no". So, I told them that it looked like they were out the money and the furniture. Within 30 minutes, they called Dwayne (I guess they were tired of dealing with me) and asked where they could pick up the furniture.

We moved into a different apartment together, and we were finally a family. He wanted me to quit working and stay home with the kids, and I was more than happy to. Around November of that year, I was planning to leave the home health care service. I really did enjoy what I did, but it was getting difficult with all of Charles' buddies hanging around, and Charles was unable to pay me more, so it was just not worth it anymore. I loved the old folks and became close to a few of them, but it got too hard when they died. It broke my heart when I saw the way some of their families treated them.

On my last day at work, Dwayne had been out of town working for the day and called me when he returned. He said that we owed Gordan a new truck. "What?" He said that he had fallen asleep at the wheel and hit a barricade, spun around and hit the other one, tearing up the racks on the truck. Dwayne, Gordan and another worker were all three alright, but it scared the crap out of everyone. For a while after that, Dwayne said that Gordan would freak out any time Dwayne would hit a curb.

Charles was a nice guy, and he understood why I was leaving; he thanked me for all I had done to help his company and wished Dwayne and I the best. He later moved it down to "the valley", which was near the Texas/Mexico border where his parents lived.

After a while, Dwayne and I discussed getting married. He kept telling me that a piece of paper would not prevent him from leaving, if he really wanted to. I knew that God must have a plan for us and prayed about it for a time. We decided to get married and set the date for July 12, 1986. We lived together for two years prior; I wanted to make our union legal and right in the eyes of God. I knew that Dwayne was not a Christian, but I knew that he loved me and we would make it work.

Dwayne understood right off the bat that I put God first, and I would not stop going to church just because he didn't go with me. He was alright with that. I hoped that over the years he would see just what an influence my faith had in everything I did. He just never understood how we (my family) could be so religious when we grew up the way we did. I tried to tell him that it was because of our faith that we survived everything.

Getting Married

When we met with the preacher about the arrangements for our wedding, it was almost a comedy show. Dwayne's mother, stepdad and dad would be there, and we needed to figure out where everyone would sit. When it got to my side, I think that the preacher just about fell out. I had my mother, stepdad, biological father and foster parents. Annette made both the wedding and groom's cakes. Joni sang, Anne was the flower girl, and Jeremy was the ring bearer. Greig was his best man, and Sue was my maid of honor. I made Sue and Anne's dress. I found mine at a discount at the bridal shop. Since I had been married before I couldn't wear white, so I chose a pink and maroon dress.

Dwayne told me later that the day of the wedding, there had been someone attacked in the church earlier in the day. I am so glad he didn't tell me until later. Daddy walked me down the aisle. In retrospect, I wish Daddy Deardan had. What do you do when you have three dads that you really wanted to walk you down the aisle?

We had a nice crowd, around 50 friends and relatives. When it came time to throw the bouquet, no one wanted to catch it. It took me three tries to get them to cooperate. I guess no one wanted to get married next. Some just like being bachelorettes. Then it was time for Dwayne to toss the garter. Same thing, no one wanted to catch it. It became a joke by then. After the wedding, Betsy took the kids to her house and we dropped Bert, Dwayne's dad, at the airport; we hit the road. Dwayne wouldn't tell me where we were going. We just got on I-10 and headed west. We wound up in San Antonio and checked into the Hyatt on the river walk. We spent the weekend walking the river walk, taking a carriage ride through town, and listening to the zydeco music of an old gentleman on the street. We headed to Aquarena Springs for a boat ride, watched the swimming pig, then we traveled to Natural Bridge Caverns. We even hit the river in New Braunfels. We did a lot in just a few days. We got back to Houston, and Dwayne finally admitted that he had no plans for our honeymoon, it just happened. Since then, I have learned that there is just no telling where we would end up when we got into the truck.

Amarillo Glass

In 1983, Dwayne and Gordan started a glass company. Just after we got together, I helped him send out bid requests and contact general contractors. I talked with Daddy Deardan and asked him to let his contacts know about the glass company and maybe help us get on the bid lists. He let several know, but as it turns out, Dwayne and Daddy knew some of the same people. Getting to know Gordan was interesting; he and his wife Iva were from Yugoslavia, and we all became friends as well as business partners. Their daughter was a few months younger than Anne, and they played together whenever we were at the shop. After a year or so, he sold his shares back to Gordan. He continued to work with Gordan for years.

When we were in the middle of moving into the second apartment, we stayed with Gordan and Iva in their apartment. They definitely had different customs and sayings than us. Iva had no idea what coupons were for. She started collecting them and Gordan was mad at me for that. Anne had a runny nose, so I asked Iva for a tissue. She brought me a sanitary pad. We both laughed. She always fed her daughter around eight at night, and I fed my kids a lot earlier. I put them down to bed about 8:30, so Dwayne and I could spend some quiet time together. My schedule was just too rigorous for Iva. When Anne went to the restroom by herself, Iva thought I was nuts. I told her that Anne could wipe her own fanny and didn't need me to do it for her. She was three at the time. They never disciplined Adrijana, and it drove me crazy. I would discipline my kids and that would upset Iva. After a few days, I couldn't handle things there, so I went to stay a few days with my mother since she lived close to my job. I figured that we would be moving in a few days into an apartment anyway.

We moved into a place on the west side of town. It was actually just a couple of miles from Betsy's house.

We saw each other a little bit more often in a family setting instead of just at lunch while at work.

The apartments were nice, and there were a lot of kids, so mine had others to play with. In the summer months, I would keep them all busy with different activities at the pool, and once, we even collected food around the apartments for the needy. I kind of became the unofficial activities director. It kept all the kids occupied, and I had fun. We played games and had relays in the pool; we even did a scavenger hunt. We all divided into teams and went for the hunt.

The glass shop was starting to get more business, and it got to where the only way I saw Dwayne was to go to work with him. One day we were on a stage weatherproofing the glass, caulking the exterior of the building. After lunch, we all three got back on the stage and hooked up our safety belts and headed back up. Well, my rope was an old one, and when that happens, the rope gets a little swollen. It would not go through the lanyard holder that slips up the rope with you and wouldn't let you fall back down. It is sort of a brake. My rope was tied off to the metal grate down below, but my lanyard would not go up the rope so easy; it was about to pull me off the stage. I kept yelling at Dwayne and he'd say, "Hang on we're almost there." Well I was just about to hit the quick release when he noticed that I was almost hanging over the top rail of the stage. We got a big laugh out of it later, and I still won't let him live that one down.

Another job I went to was in Baytown. We were scraping concrete off the side metal so clips could be welded on. We hired a local boy to help, so he was working on one side and me on the other. When some men from the general contractors showed up, they were asking me some questions. The boy stopped working and came over to see what was up. I looked at him and told him that we weren't paying him to stand around. He went back to work. When we got back to the shop, Gordan was ribbing me about being the bad ass woman on the job. Men just aren't used to having women for bosses or seeing them on construction jobs. It is still a man's world.

96

We had a Christmas party in the shop for our vendors and clients. The city was working on the streets around the shop, so there was a huge pile of crushed up asphalt and dirt across the street. Gordan knew I liked to shoot, so we had a women's shooting match, using the pile of dirt as a back drop.

Off and on, Dwayne and Gordan would get into an argument like a married couple. Dwayne would stomp off and stay gone a week or two, and then he'd go back. Well one of those arguments led us to Round Rock, just north of the Austin area.

Round Rock

Dwayne found a job in Corpus Christi and decided that it was just as far from Round Rock as it was from Houston, plus the Austin area was really nice, so we made the move. We visited with some friends, JW and Robin, who also lived in Round Rock. JW and Dwayne had been friends for a long time. They knew of a house in his area for rent, so we went and looked in the windows because we were unable to get the agent to come let us in. We called him again the following Monday and rented it, just about sight unseen.

We were on the move again. This made move number 27 for me. Being uprooted that many times in one's life can be a little unsettling. The house was nice and felt like home. Anne started all day kindergarten, and we made some friends in the neighborhood. We were close to Austin, so we would go on little hiking trips on the greenbelts and drive around the hill country. Texas has some really beautiful country, from the flatness of Houston to hill country in the middle of the state to mountins in the southern Big Bend area.

Shortly after moving to Round Rock, Dwayne got laid off from the Corpus job, but found another in Austin. In between jobs, we got a Rottweiler puppy. He was so cute. We planned to take him to the mountains with us, so I made a pack for him to carry his own food, water and possibly our tent. We would train him with a smaller pack and less weight on our hikes on the greenbelts.

When Wiley was only eight months old, he attacked a girl on her bike, so he had to get quarantined. He just barely broke the skin on her leg. Apparently, dogs are attracted to the feet on the pedals of the bike. She was alright, but because it happened off our property, he had to get quarantined. We took him for walks while sequestered, and when the ten days were up, I brought him back home. That day he almost went through the screen door at Anne. I just don't know what happened to him. That same week Jeremy was playing with him and his bone, tossing it for him to fetch. It landed in his water bowl, so he decided to eat some food. When Jeremy reached down to get the bone out of the water, Wiley attacked him and knocked him off the stoop. He had been bitten in the arm and on the face. The doctor stitched him up, but we had to get rid of Wiley. We gave him to a man that was not planning to have a family. We hated to see him go, but what else could we do? If we had him put down, I found out that the state would have to do a rabies test on him. In order to do that, they have to kill him and they send his head in for the tests. So, we gave him away.

Burn

The first time Dwayne was out of work, he was out walking the dog when the pot I had been cooking with exploded; I got burned on my left arm, face and torso. They told me that I was burned over 30% of my body with 3rd degree burns. We had no insurance, of course, so we went to an urgent clinic for emergency treatment. We just didn't know where to go, and this place was really close. Dwayne had taken me in a sheet with frozen hamburger on my breast. The doctor laughed and handed him the hamburger and told him, "Here is dinner." I always flattened my hamburger in the bag and froze it. It was the best choice to cover the most area on my body.

We went home with me looking like a wrapped-up mummy. Dwayne left to get my prescriptions, and asked the neighbor to look for the kids coming home from school, to not let them see me until he got back. Malinda didn't catch them, and I remember the kids, especially Anne, freaking out. Malinda came over and took them to her house. With us going to an urgent clinic, the heaviest drugs they are allowed to give you is something like Tylenol 4. I felt like I was in a floating state. I could hear everything, but couldn't respond. I was totally out of it.

The daily treatments were excruciatingly painful. They scrubbed, scraped and pulled skin off of me. Dwayne was there with me through most of it. One treatment, he didn't go with me, and they gave me a shot of something. I was reading my book when about twenty minutes later I was out, but not totally out. I could feel some, but it was like the pain receptors in my brain were firing on delay. The doctor told me that I was lucky to have come here because he had worked for three years in Argentina in a burn hospital. After a while of debriding two separate areas, I had to get him to stop. It was just too much. When he kept saying, "just a little bit more", I couldn't handle it and I punched him. He rolled back on his stool. I apologized, but I did tell him to stop. He did after that.

The following visit Dwayne went with me, at my urging. When they gave me the shot, the doctor didn't wait long enough and started to poke at me. I told him that it hurt too much, to wait, but he kept on. I told him that he better quit, or I would hit him again. Dwayne said that if I didn't, he would. The doctor started laughing and said, "No need, she will and has." He stopped and didn't do anymore that day.

I prayed every day for God to take the pain away and for healing. He was with me through it all, I know, and I endured all the pain and suffering because of my faith.

For two years, I was supposed to stay out of the sun. I healed up pretty good with no apparent signs of the burns. Later, when we took our hiking trip, Dwayne told me that when the doctor was pulling away dead skin, he explained to him how the skin grows and why he had to pull off the dead skin. He thought the doctor was pulling away new skin. I have been thinking that maybe the doctor was one of those Nazis that escaped to Argentina; maybe I was right.

Sometime after that, I got into some poison ivy. I am very allergic to it, so I got it bad. All of the new skin was a deep maroon color, and it itched something fierce. The skin under my chin was hanging down like an old person's. I went to the doctor and got a prednisone shot, and it all cleared up pretty well. I looked like something out of a horror movie.

First Hiking Trip

On our first trip to the mountains in Wyoming, I saw more of the state at that time than I did while living there for two and a half years. We stayed in Dubois for a day or two and re-packed our packs. Dwayne took us around to show us some really beautiful country. Wyoming has some of the most beautiful country I'd ever seen. When driving around, one tends to just see the dirt and scrub brush. But when driving or hiking into the mountains, it opens up to the most beautiful scenery.

We tend to take many things for granted, but when hiking, one must revise their own actions. Going to the restroom is one of those such actions. I asked Dwayne what to do. He told me to just burn the paper. I told him, after my first time, that the paper just doesn't burn, when it is all wet. When I had to go number two, I was at a loss. I was to find a rock, not too big or too small, roll it over, do my business and roll the rock back. Well, it took me almost ten minutes to find the right size. They were either too small or way too big, and I was on the side of a mountain with an incline. I finally found the right size and squatted, and my rock rolled down the hill. I was so frustrated. I had to find another rock. Biodegradable products are a necessity in the mountains. There is a well-known saying when hiking, "Pack in and pack out what you have and don't leave a trace." Just don't turn over many rocks.

We saw beautiful waterfalls and elk, and the water was cold and beautifully clear. The kids were fishing, continuing to catch fish about four to five inches long, not long enough for a meal. Finally, we told them to keep the next one they caught. It was about seven inches long, so it was doable. Dwayne took it down a small cliff next to the water to clean it, and it slipped into the water. He was able to snag it with a pole and tried again. He had it gutted and cleaned and was bringing it up to me when it fell into the water again. He snagged it again, and we finally got it into the pan. The kids refused to eat it. Anne said that it was too pretty, and it was her friend. Dwayne and I ate it.

We only packed in one change of clothes, so we decided to wash what we had on and hang the clothes up to dry. Not long after that it started raining. We had to cover our packs and grab the trail mix and run to the tent. One should never eat in the tent, but what were we to do when it just didn't stop raining for three days? We had to cook, eat and sleep in the tent. For entertainment between rain showers, we fed the chipmunks and squirrels our trail mix, just outside the tent. We taught the kids every dice and card game we could come up with.

We had a great time, but we were really glad to see the Jeep at the trail head. We visited many sites around Wyoming and Colorado on the way home. We even stopped in Cheyenne and I showed Dwayne around F.E. Warren Air Force Base. Dwayne thought the missile carriers were pretty cool. The horses and wagons at the Frontier Days Celebration were the kids' favorites. This would not be our only trip hiking in Wyoming or Colorado.

Plumbing

Dwayne's uncle, Duke, had a plumbing business in Austin. I went to work with him on several jobs. He encouraged me to take my National Plumbing Exam for a Journeyman's license. We didn't do any gas plumbing in the service, so he tutored me in that area. I had been taught ground up construction in the Air Force training program, but we almost never did any new construction. All of that would be contracted out to civilian contractors. I studied and prayed about it for a long time. I prayed that God would open my mind to what I needed to remember. I finally scheduled my test and paid the $400. I was so nervous. This was a man's world, and they didn't like women intervening in their space.

I showed up for the test, and if looks were any indication, I was in trouble. They really didn't want me there. I took the test and felt pretty good about it. I was always good at sweating joints in cast iron, and the written test went pretty well, or so I thought. I got the results later and I failed. I asked them where I went wrong, and they refused to tell me. I just needed to pay the $400 and take it again. Some had told me that they had to take it four times to finally pass. I was stubborn and wanted satisfaction. During the test, one of the men that proctored the test seemed to be constantly hovering over me and not anyone else. I accused them of being sexist and demanded to know where I had gone wrong. He finally told me that my water heater flame was not correct and one other thing, which I forgot.

I retested and passed. I was one of the first 125 women in the state of Texas to get my Journeyman's license. Now finding a job would be another story. I tried several companies, and no one wanted a female plumber. I worked with Duke for a while, but he just didn't have enough work to keep me busy.

Laid Off Second Time

Dwayne got laid off again, and there were no other jobs in the Austin area. It was like someone turned off the switch for any further development. He went back to work with Gordan in Houston, so he had to commute back and forth. We wanted to wait until the kids finished school before moving back. He would stay with Annette in her townhouse, since she lived just a couple of miles from work. We paid for any increase on the bills and helped out a little more besides. She told him to not expect her to cook for him. So he ate out all the time. Dwayne doesn't cook, in fact, he would probably burn water.

When he first moved in there, she told him to be careful of the downstairs toilet and make sure that it stopped running. He didn't, and it flooded her house as well as the neighbor's house. We had to pay for someone to come in and dry out everything in both places. Then, the air conditioning went out, so we paid to have that repaired. Dwayne was starting to rethink this arrangement, but nothing else went bad.

He was having trouble eating because he had to have his wisdom teeth taken out. Annette took pity on him and made him a shake one night. He would tell me how he could eat his scallops. He would have to cut them up into little bitty bites and push them into his mouth. Poor thing, I felt bad for him, but this too, did pass.

Dwayne was bad about speeding, and one time when he got pulled over, he was told that he had a suspended license. He didn't know about it, so the officer let him off. He had to get an expensive proof of insurance and get a limited driving permit, just so he could work. I called the courthouse and asked them what I could do without getting a lawyer involved. They let me come and get a redacted claim from them, telling me to just follow it. I did, and at one point, it said that I had to list the counties that he would be working in. I called and talked with a judge to ask his advice since Dwayne worked all over Texas. What should I put down? He told me to put "Texas" in that spot.

When Dwayne went to court, I had all the paperwork in order for him to get a restricted permit. The judge looked at the paperwork and asked if his lawyer was present. He said that he didn't have one. The judge asked who did his paperwork. He told him that his wife did it.

"Is she a lawyer?" the judge asked.

"No sir," Dwayne said. The judge wanted to know how I knew what to do and who told me to put down Texas in place of a county. Dwayne told him that I had talked to another judge, and he advised me. Dwayne came away with his permit. He was allowed to drive anywhere in Texas between 3 a.m. and 3 p.m. But of course, he had to drive after 3 p.m. since he came home on Fridays after work.

For the kid's birthdays, we usually had a party either the weekend before or just after. Tim was in San Angelo, Texas, for training so I asked him if he wanted to come to Jeremy's birthday that following weekend. I told him to let me know ASAP. He just complained about how to get there. I told him to catch a hop to Bergstrom AFB in Austin, and I could pick him up. He could stay at the base there. He never called, so on Friday, we packed up after the kids got home from school and headed to Houston. We stayed at Annette's house and had a family party there. When we returned to Round Rock, there was a message from Tim saying that he wanted to come out and asking why I didn't call him back. I called him to say that he should not have waited until the last minute to call me. I didn't wait around for him anymore. He was in Texas for three months and never came over to see the kids.

The landlord told us to not send any more checks and that the bank would be getting in touch with us. He had filed for bankruptcy, so it would be handled through the courts. After a few months, a banker did come around and was surprised that someone was living in the house. He said that we had to move out, so they could sell it. I told him that we needed a few more months until school was out; we were moving back to Houston. He agreed, and I asked him if he knew that there was a secondary mortgage on the house, He didn't and had to look into it. We got about seven months of free rent and were ready to move when school was out.

We had been going to Houston on the weekends to find a house to purchase. Nothing seemed to fit Dwayne. He kept complaining about having to do too much to the house, like replacing lights or wall plugs. I didn't see the big deal. We were running out of time and needed someplace to move.

Move to Katy

It was June 1st, and I had the whole house packed and ready to move. Dwayne had been looking for a house to rent; he got lost and came across this house in the country, sort of. It was on two acres and had an old house with a 1200 square foot warehouse. I could open my ceramic shop in it. He kept joking about this house, comparing it to the one we lived at in the Heights. He had me scared. He showed up with our friend, Red, and the rack truck. We moved the first load down to Katy into the warehouse. There was no power, so we unloaded everything into the warehouse. He took me through the house with a cigarette lighter. I was so upset. It had walls like a trailer, soft like you could put your hand through them, and each room had a different type and color carpet. It had one bathroom and three bedrooms.

We got all moved in, and it turned out to be one of the best moves for us. I was able to start my ceramic shop in the warehouse. Dwayne put a glass storefront on one side, and I started building my supplies little by little. I had fun with it.

The kids and I joined a local church and the youth group. I think they enjoyed it, and I joined the choir. It was not too big and that made it more friendly and personal. I really felt at home there.

I'm not much of a dog person. My mother always had cats, so I guess it was in my genes. In spite of that, we soon got another Rottweiler and named him Wiley II. This time we got him at six weeks old instead of nine. I think it was better. He grew to be a great dog. Every animal has its own personality, and Wiley developed into a great guard dog as well as a great companion. He loved pizza, and once the pizza delivery man came, Wiley rushed out of the shop to meet him. The guy just about had a heart attack. I told him to just reach inside and give him a slice. They were buddies from then on.

We had two cats when we got Wiley. The kitten, Sammy, would try to become friends with Wiley, and they chased each other around. Of course, Wiley grew up faster than Sammy, and he would get on top of the truck tire to be eye level with the dog. They were so funny. Sammy let him have it in the snout a few times.

The kids liked to skateboard down the street, so they would let Wiley pull them down the street instead. Dwayne built a buggy for him to pull since that was the history of the breed. They were milk cart dogs in Germany. But when we hooked him up to it, he just didn't like that "thing" getting too close to his behind. They were also herding dogs. There were times we would catch him in the field across the street herding the cattle.

On our street, there was only one other house and a trailer park next door. The streets beyond our house were developed, but they never built houses. This was a good play area for us to walk the dog, shoot our .22 caliber rifle in the bayou, or take a canoe into the sandpit full of water. There were even some dirt hills to play on with our little four-wheeler.

That Honda four-wheeler was some of the best money we ever spent. We would take it to the beach, and Dwayne would try to drown it, but that didn't work. We had a small utility trailer and would take Anne's Brownie troop on rides around the yard and down the street. Since we were on two acres, we turned the back acre into a 4-wheel track for the kids to ride and stay close to home. When the streets would ice up, we would go skating there.

Started Ceramic Shop

I started my ceramic business in the warehouse. I wanted a shop like we had in the military, where one could rent the molds for twenty cents or so and pour one's own greenware. When I got out of the service and moved back to Houston, I had called several shops to see if they did this. They all thought I was nuts. So, I started my own store. I sold greenware and taught classes and even did birthday parties. It was great having my own business, especially since I was able to stay at home with the kids.

We had to come up with a name for the business. One weekend, we had some friends over. Someone had brought over an old film that we had all seen in high school, titled "Reefer Madness". It was supposed to turn youngsters away from the evils of marijuana. In the movie, everyone went to "Mae's Place" to get reefer. It became a joke and also the name of my shop, "Mae's Place Ceramics".

I got pretty good at it, and even invited the owner of our art supply out to my shop. This shop sold everything for the crafty person, from paints to glass. He had just purchased our local ceramic supply store and didn't have anyone to train his employees. I suggested that whoever was going to work in the ceramic supply department needed to be trained. He hired me on as a consultant. I had a good time, and it helped out our ceramic community because the employees didn't know how to help anyone, not knowing anything about ceramics.

I liked the challenge of pouring the tough pieces, so after a while, others in the ceramic community would bring me their tough molds. I would figure out the best way to pour them, and of course, I would pour myself a few pieces to sell, which made up for the time I spent figuring it out.

We had a big ceramic show at the Astro Arena, and I liked to put pieces in the competition for different areas of interests. One of my vendors was the folks from APTII. I used their product in a few pieces. One could take the product and add it to the slip (mud) and add underglazes, then dip silk flowers in it. When fired, they would take on the shape of the silk and have color. Then, after firing the first time, I would arrange them in a basket or on top of a ceramic cake cover and glaze them. When fired, they fused together. I would take a thicker batch of colored slip and put it through a cake decorator bag and pipe it onto the cake like icing. My cake cover won first prize. The cake, and a basket I'd done, were published in a couple of our national ceramic magazines. I loved doing ceramics. I got really good at it and learned all sorts of techniques. The business did pretty well.

The kids were always messing with me, saying that Santa was on the phone or something like that. One day they told me that Don Nelson was on the phone. Don Nelson was a host of our local "Good Morning Houston" show. They did a "Dialing for Dollars" segment, and when I answered the phone and realized that it really was him, all I could think was, "oh crap I didn't listen to the show for the numbers", not realizing that it was well after the time slot for the show. He had received my recipes for the Guamanian Lumpia and Finadene that I had sent in for their cooking segment. He wanted to tape it the following week; I was so excited.

Dwayne wanted to paint the kitchen and clean up the place. He was getting a bit too over-zealous. We bought a video camera, and he followed me around all weekend long. I had to get the "crazy me" out of my system. I just wanted to stick my tongue out at the camera or make some stupid face.

The time came, and I let the kids stay home from school and invited a neighbor over. We would all get to be on the show. I had to have one batch prepared, and then we would go through, on camera, the cooking process. I didn't want to overdo the ceramics, but I did want to show my stuff on camera, so I just had a couple of pieces around. I had on a shirt with my shop and phone number on it. Little did I know that it wouldn't show up on camera? Neither did the white walls. No need to paint after all. I had this awful looking perm in my hair and boy was it curly. When we finished the cooking part, we sat down to the table, and Don asked me if I had any more finished ceramics. I told him "of course" and I went to the shop and brought in more. He introduced everyone and showed off my ceramics and talked about the shop. He even had my phone number displayed across the bottom of the screen. I couldn't have paid for that kind of advertising. I got calls for a year. For the immediate moment, I got calls about the recipes, and where did I get my fryer, and so on? I got my first commercial account from it as well. It aired on Thursday one week at nine in the morning and six in the morning the following week. Good thing I recorded it because I couldn't watch it due to the phone ringing off the hook.

When I had been open just a year, I decided to look into going into the Reserves. I just hadn't gotten that out of my system yet. With Clinton being elected, though, I opted not to go back in. Besides, I had the momentum going with the shop and really didn't want to stop at that time for fear of losing the shop all together.

I liked the flexibility of working from home. Crafts are my thing and this fit my niche perfectly. Most of the customers that would come became friends. It was a comfortable shop to come to and hang out and paint, or to work on one's crafts at any stage of production. Sometimes, it was like the old-time quilt parties, or as one might say, hen party.

Disney

In 1988, we took a trip to Disney for Christmas. As we headed that way, I read an unofficial guide to Disney. It gave us routes to take during certain times of the day to avoid the crowds. On the radio, however, we start hearing about the Christmas parade at Disney and decided to avoid the bigger crowd; we headed to Cape Canaveral, then eventually Key West.

We camped just outside of Cape Canaveral. The kids got a real kick out of the raccoons coming up to us. We fed them, even though we were not supposed to. The following day, we did the bus tour of Kennedy Space Center, then headed south. My brother-in-law, Jacque, told us that we could stay on his boat in Key Largo. It smelled horrible, so we decided to continue on to Key West. We made it there before nightfall and got a hotel room. The next day, we went exploring. Dwayne lived there as a child with his mother and step-dad, who was in the Navy. The only apartment building that was still standing on base was the one he lived in, so it was cool for him to see that. He remembered some of the sights and reminisced about the time during the Cuban Missile Crisis.

It took so long to get to the final key, Key West. I just wanted to drive around the island and look at everything, including Hemingway's house. We didn't go in and tour, but we did drive by it. The "Southern Most End of the United States" was probably the coolest spot on the island, knowing that you are in the southern most spot in the contiguous United States. Of course, Guam is probably the southern-most point of the total US properties and territories.

We drove back to Disney and had a great time. We camped out most nights, and we spent one night at Greig's house in Tampa. It was good to see him and his wife. One night, we stayed in a hotel so we could do laundry. We traveled back along the coast and stopped off at a couple of other beaches. Even though it was

December, and the water was too cold to get into, it was nice to see the prettier beaches. We stopped off at the USS Alabama for a tour. We saw a crocodile swimming by the ship. The kids got a kick out of the ship and the big guns. Anne coveted her USS Alabama Sailor hat. She wore it everywhere.

We arrived back home where Dwayne's friend, John, had been house-sitting for us. This was probably the most fun vacation I had ever had. At least in the top two so far because Wyoming was also pretty cool, but getting rained in for a few days was not exactly comparable to Disney World.

JB Winzlett Membranes

Dwayne changed careers and started working for JB Winzlett Membrane Systems. It was an oil field related business. One Christmas, Dwayne had to work in Colorado on the west side of the Rockies. I was going to go to Annette's in New Braunfels and told him to call me when he made it to Denver because I know how they close the passes sometimes when they get too much snow. I even put the phone numbers in his shave kit and his wallet. Well, he didn't call, and before I left the house, I turned off the heat, not expecting anything too cold between then and Christmas. Oops, we ended up getting an ice storm, and they closed Interstate 10 from Houston to San Antonio; our pipes froze.

I got a call from his friend, Red, saying that Dwayne was mad because he couldn't get a hold of me. He would go pick him up at the airport. When Dwayne called me, he told me the pipes were frozen, and the house was really cold. I was sorry, but it wasn't expected and why didn't he call me anyway? He wanted me to come home then. I told him that I would come home the next day because the interstate was closed. He told me, "I buy you a big gun, a big dog and a big four-wheel drive so you can go anywhere." The conversation started to get heated, and I hung up. The next morning, we got up and came home. The roads were clear all the way home. By the time we got home, the house was well heated, and he met me at the truck with a present for me, a pair of earrings. He apologized and told me that he had lost the phone number; that is why he didn't call when he got to Denver.

Dwayne worked all over the world. He went to Taiwan, Australia and Argentina. The first time he went to Argentina, we were out of touch for a few weeks. I thought I was going to go crazy. When he was in the States, he would call every night. When he was finally able to call, he told me about the heat pump.

115

There was a community barracks or house where the foreign workers stayed when they were there. There was a living room, and he said that it was really cold. He couldn't figure out how to make this air conditioner work. He tried several switches to no avail. The following night, someone new had come in and showed him the switches marked "caliente" and "frio". Caliente meant hot or heat. He felt stupid.

There was a local woman there to teach the workers to speak English. She would sit on the floor next to the couch by Dwayne. He called me one time asking since I had been in other cultures before, was this woman flirting or was it just their culture? She was sitting really close to him while he was on the couch, and she would lean over his lap to get something. I told him that was flirting and she better get back. He just laughed.

Guamanian men and women would walk around hand in hand with friends of the same sex, and it didn't mean they were homosexual. They were very friendly, but it sounded like that woman was getting a little more flirty than desired.

On one other trip to Argentina he was working in another region and had been gone for almost 30 days. I was about out of my mind missing him. He finally called and said that he was heading back, but wanted to stop off at the other camp and take this woman, who taught English, to dinner. My green-eyed monster came out. I wanted him home and I meant right then. He did go by there, but she was not there, so he came on home.

When he went to Taiwan, he was unsure of the food there. He said that it looked weird. I told him of the food in Guam with neon green and purple stuff that came out of the sea. I didn't eat it, just too slimy for me. He told me that he tried some, but didn't like it. The following night, the restaurant had a hamburger for him.

Jeremy and Anne really enjoyed living in Katy. We were able to do some really cool stuff around the property. My friend, Doug, had brought his canoe over to store with us. When we got some heavy rain, the yard in back of the house would flood, and the kids would get into the canoe and pretend they were canoeing down the river.

My brother-in-law brought his boat over to store in our back field. Unfortunately for him, it got stuck in the wet ground. Dwayne hooked it up to his GMC, but to no avail. I hooked up our four-wheel drive Ford and pulled them both out. It was funny, and of course, we got bragging rights with the Ford. The GMC was a company truck, so everyone at Dwayne's office heard about it too. That property had once been a dairy farm, so the ground was really soft and low in elevation. It flooded all the time.

The ditch across the street was deeper than your average ditch. The asphalt on the street in front of the house was buckled up, causing big bumps. Whenever big trucks would go by, our house would rattle. About once a month, a car would end up in the ditch across the street. With no development down the street, the cars and trucks would use our road as a cut off to avoid the lights down on the main street.

The trailer park next door had a major leak in some of their plumbing and storm drains, so it would flow into our yard and come up to our ankles. I complained to the park and the environmental department. The county came and fixed the problem. In doing so, they had to dig out the ditches down our street. I talked them into dumping some of the dirt into our yard. MISTAKE! It smelled to high heaven. We borrowed my brother-in-law, Jacque's, little Bobcat and plowed it all down, then put sod all over the front yard. That took the smell out and we had a nice green lawn.

I had a friend named Cindy Marrow who had Muscular Dystrophy. She was an inspiration to me. She was wheelchair bound, but that didn't stop her. She liked to do ceramics, and that is how we met. I liked her right away. She also sewed and did a multitude of crafts, including knitting with an automatic knitting machine. She made me a sweater that I still have to this day. The sleeves are a little short, but I wear it from time to time, thinking of her. She also made Anne a bridal gown for a Barbie. She had it all set up nice with a bouquet and hair

117

decoration. We became real close. She would give the shirt off her back to help anyone she could.

She drove a van with hand controls, so she was able to get around quite well. One time, she had an accident, and her wheelchair and van were totaled. The insurance would not replace her chair with the type she had, which was an electric one. She tried to get the MD Jerry's Kids foundation to help her, but they said that she was too old for their criteria. She tried several others, but to no avail. She was grounded with no van or electric wheelchair. She did finally get another van, but the wheelchair was still a problem. I felt really bad for her. She died at the young age of forty-nine.

Living in Katy for six years was the longest I lived anywhere. I felt like I had accomplished something, but it was time to get our own place. We looked to build a house and found out that we needed a lot more money than we had to do that, so we looked to purchase an existing home. Dwayne didn't want me to close my shop, so we couldn't move into Katy proper because I'd have to rent a storefront or own my own property. Nothing like that in Katy proper, and besides there was already a ceramic business there. We looked in Waller, not too far from my dad. I really wasn't looking forward to being too close to him, but it wouldn't be too bad. So around 1993-1994, we looked around for something with a high elevation. We would drive around the different areas that we were interested in and get the TOPO maps to look at the elevations. Waller was 250 feet in elevation where we were only 90 feet in Katy. We just got tired of getting stuck in our own back yard.

Move to Waller

After Daddy died in 1994, we found a place that had a warehouse that I could move my ceramic business into. It was a little larger than the one I had. This place had a pool, which I was not too crazy about, but the kids liked it, for a while.

We moved in July and relocated the shop first thing. Dwayne put in a glass storefront for me, and we built in a wall to separate the mold storage area and the store. It looked pretty good, and again, I was able to stay at home, and I didn't have the high rent of a strip center. I just don't know how those shops can make it. They usually don't for many years. Only the shops that are located on their own property seem to stand the test of time.

We moved in and started cleaning up the pool, the yard and the shop. I didn't know what we were clearing out, but I got poison ivy really bad. I had never seen it in this form of vine before. I am very allergic and usually stay away. This looked totally different. I had it so bad that I had to wrap my arms at night because of the blisters oozing puss. I had to get a shot, and it finally cleared up. We knew after that for me to stay clear of that stuff.

When we moved in, the phone would not work, after having it turned on. That gave me the opportunity to meet the neighbors. One of my new neighbors, Cory, came to the door, and I told him that I needed to borrow his phone to call the phone company. He handed me the phone and shut the door in my face. I thought that was a bit rude. When I finished, I knocked on the door to give it back, and Pam, Cory's mom, invited me in. She was very nice, and I met the rest of the family. There was Pam, Cory, his wife Rita and their two kids, Dick and Susanna. The kids were the same ages as our kids, so that was pretty cool. They soon became best friends.

I set up the shop and started pouring greenware like crazy to fill the shelves. I started getting business, and even a few orders for finished products. Life was good.

Thinking of the best ideas to get my shop established, I wanted to join a Chamber of Commerce, but Waller didn't have one. I joined the Hempstead Chamber, and everyone in Waller wanted to know why. I told them that there was not one, so I joined Hempstead's. By January of 1995, I was looking into starting one in Waller. Some of the folks I approached asked me why I wanted to start one, and others told me that they moved out of Houston to get away from people like me. Well, they didn't have to join. I met with the mayor, who just happens to still be the mayor, or should I say is now the mayor, again. He told me that we could expand only a half mile beyond our current borders, and he didn't want that to be taken up with big businesses and their tax abetments. He wanted it filled with residential homes for a solid tax base. I told him that after only a few years' abetments, we would get a large tax base rolling in. I just didn't understand the small-town mentality. The city council was a "good ole boy" organization for sure.

I got it started, so we had our meetings at a small restaurant down the street. One time, we couldn't meet there for whatever reason. We met out at my shop, and the cars took up the whole driveway; actually, we could fit about ten cars in. Dwayne came home and was a bit put off when he couldn't get into his own driveway.

When we moved here, he told me to not talk to anyone, not to send in recipes to any shows and not to join anything. Oh well, I didn't send in any more recipes.

A murder trial had been going on for about two years. One morning, after making Dwayne's breakfast and lunch, I was lying on the couch watching the news. They talked about this trial and showed the defendant's face this time. When they said his name, Kurt Mare, it clicked. I knew him from high school. He was in JROTC with me and dated my friend, Sue. We all three hung out together a lot. I couldn't believe it. He was sentenced to death and went to Huntsville to death row. I wrote to him and finally went to see him. He told me that they didn't arrest him until about a year after the fact. He was accused of going into his neighbor's house and killing two little girls in their bedroom while their brother was in the living room watching television. He swore that he was innocent and that one day the DNA would prove it. They did not allow DNA evidence in court yet. He said that his wife divorced him and his twin daughters were at Texas A & M, so they didn't have much to do with him anymore. It was a very sad situation. I felt so bad for him whether he was guilty or not. He had been my friend.

Anne wanted to play football in seventh and eighth grade. Previously, there had been a lawsuit against another school in a small town north of Houston, so the coaches here knew that they couldn't refuse her, but they did send home letters asking if we were sure that we wanted her to play. It turns out that she was pretty good, and the coaches liked that she seemed to encourage the boys to do better. Or at least they got shamed into doing better.

Whenever I would go to her games, it was fun to listen to the parents when they would realize that there was a girl on the team. They'd say, "I can't believe that her parents would let her play," "her parents are crazy to let her play," and more. I would just tell them that she played in the neighborhood, and at least with organized football, she wore pads. She gave as good as she got. We didn't let her play in high school. The boys just got too big. Instead, she did track and wound up hurting her ankle. She did letter in varsity her freshman year.

Jeremy tried playing football one summer when the school started practicing. He had a hard time with it, and I think his heart just wasn't into it. He decided to play the saxophone in the band. He was pretty good with the sax. He is musically inclined and real artistic, as well. He was always drawing something. I would find papers around with a scribbled drawing on it. I kept some of them. He would like to take apart his bike and paint it a new color every so often. He was quieter than Anne and seemed to express himself through either his music or his art.

Anne took to the country living better than Jeremy; he just wanted to go back to Katy. There weren't many kids in our neighborhood. They both hung out with the kids next door. Cory and Rita would take them with their family to Summerville for camping and boating. Anne and Susanna became best friends until Jeremy started dating her, then the friendship got a little strained. Jeremy and Susanna became more involved and planned to get married.

We had some pretty good neighbors; I didn't have many while living in Katy. I developed a friendship with Laura and her family. She and Thomas have three children. I met them through our church. I was a Sunday school teacher with only one child in class. We were working on hand puppets, but it is hard to do a full production with only two people. Soon Laura's kids would start coming, then a few friends of theirs. I had more in my class and decided to let the kids pick their favorite Bible stories and we would act them out. I brought in old clothes and robes. It was fun, but I had an idea. The church was going to renovate the sanctuary, so I got permission to put on a play with the children. We could decorate the sanctuary like a real stage.

We worked on putting together skits from their favorite stories and made it into a production. The skits were made to sort of leapfrog throughout the production. Some of the skits were in parts so we mixed them up. We did a scene of one part, then did another story, then went back to the second scene of the previous story. It was a lot of fun. We titled it "God Has a Sense of Humor Too". I stapled white Christmas lights on the ceiling for the creation of light and put a pulley system to raise the land out of the ocean. I had the two smallest children carry a huge fish pillow across the stage for when God gave us fish. All of us walked across stage, wearing animal pool floaties, when God created the animals that walked the earth. We used the SS Minnow as our model for when Jesus calmed the seas from the boat.

By the time we put on the production, we had eleven children and fifteen church members coming to church. The kids painted the scenery out of cardboard boxes from refrigerators. It all turned out great. We had a full house and it appeared that everyone had a great time.

When it was over, our attendance increased to eighty-eight. I had started the MYF with twenty-five kids of all ages.

During the MYF meetings, I would let them listen to Christian music and play games for the first thirty minutes. Afterwards, we ate and had a devotional. One of the kids wanted to bring in a Christian Rap CD to listen to. The following Sunday, I had another woman helping me. She heard the rap music and thought it was bad music or something of the sort. Her husband was president of the church board, so they reported to the others that I was letting the kids listen to evil music. I never got the chance to address the issue and explain that it was Christian music. I guess she didn't listen to the words. They fired me from the volunteer position of Youth Director. I sent a letter of resignation for that position as well as Sunday School Chairman and teacher. I figured that if they didn't trust me to work with the kids during the MYF, then I shouldn't continue as Sunday school teacher. The board didn't know how to take it. The minister was a friend of mine. When I attended church as a teenager, he was the minister. I also worked for him as part time secretary. He tried to help me out, but he said that they wouldn't listen. He felt terrible because he knew me well and knew that I would not have let this happen. I had done so much for the church and its youth.

After this, I became sour at the church and all churches. I went on a searching mission to find where I would be comfortable again. I needed the church. I went to another large church in our area, but they didn't run it like the regular church that I had been to. They had no one there during the week, that I could talk to when I needed assistance in my spiritual search. The speakers in the sanctuary were too loud and my TMJ caused my head to just about explode with the loud music; I was on a searching mission again. I like to hear congregational music. At this church, I couldn't hear the person next to me.

I wound up at another large church, though it wasn't as large as the mega church I previously attended. This was a Baptist church. It was another doctrine that I had not dealt with since I was twelve years old. I was used to Methodist or Disciples of Christ. These were the two churches that I grew up with. I had been burned previously, so I only volunteered occasionally, mostly with my photography. I took pictures at the Fall Festival and Valentine's Day. I set up my portable studio and took the kids' and couples' pictures.

This church has become my spiritual lifeline.

StarTex Marketing

Shortly after I opened the shop, a woman came in to purchase greenware and to see what all I had in stock. As it turns out, she had been buying my greenware through the shop in Katy. Her name was Cloe Boss, and we became friends right off. She was doing wholesale finished wares at shows around Texas. She warned me that I would be doing wholesale with her within two years. It was only one year when I decided that retail business was not doing very well, so I looked into joining forces with Cloe.

She owned a company called StarTex Marketing. She did angel containers and figurines, and sold them at different wholesale shows around Texas. I started doing containers, and all things Texas; such as souvenir magnets, kitchenware, and just about anything I could sponge blue and put a Bluebonnet decal on. I also did ceramic candle shades when they were in style, among other such stuff, but not just Texas related items.

We loaded up our wares and traveled to Corpus Christi, San Antonio, and Dallas. Dallas had a big show for American made products at the World Trade Center. We represented several companies at the show and got a commission. It took us a long time to set up the booths, and it was hard work. We did enjoy doing the shows. Dealing with buyers got to be pretty interesting and fun. Anne would come up to Dallas on the weekends with Dwayne to help us out at the booths.

After a few years of doing this we expanded to Kansas City, MO. That was the show from hell. I did a few pieces with the state's bird and flower, hoping to get some business in the souvenir shops. I discovered that no other state is as arrogant at Texas. We buy more of our own souvenirs than any other state. I would just call it Lone Star Pride.

After a while, I took over running StarTex and paid all the bills. Cloe's mother would join us in Dallas from time to time. We did three shows a year in Dallas. At one of our shows, a friend to Cloe's mom, Trish, would bring her wares down to sell from Oklahoma. She sold skillet magnets. When a buyer purchased $2500 worth of magnets, they got the wooden display for free. She kept bragging about selling these displays. In this show, we had five booths, plus two in the food showroom. We represented nineteen companies, and some of the owners would come and help.

During lunch, one of the ladies was telling us a joke. It was about two southern women sitting out on the porch in Alabama, Annabelle and Maribel. Annabelle would tell Maribel to look at her beautiful diamond ring her husband had given her.

Maribel would say, "That's real nice."

Then Annabelle said, "And look at this beautiful mink stole my husband just got me."

"That's real nice, Annabelle," she would reply.

"Maribel, you always talk so prim and proper, how did you get that way?" asked Annabelle.

"Well," said Maribel, "my Mama sent me to finish school."

Annabelle asked, "What did you learn there?"

"How to say, 'that's real nice' instead of 'f%$^ you'," replied Maribel.

From that day on, after lunch, every time Trish would boast about selling another display, we would reply, "That's real nice Trish."

We still laugh about that. As it turned out, Trish lost all but two of those orders for displays. When buyers get home after a show, they always trim back the orders they place. It is quite overwhelming to go to these shows. Trish thought that she should have taken over StarTex and was not really pleased with me. I just let it slide. I only had to put up with her for a week at a time.

Just after that show, the Dallas World Trade Center decided that they needed more capitol to run the center so they took on a partner from New York, Tim Little Management. They would not renew the lease of the company that we showed under. Cloe and I tried to work with the center to make us some room on one of the floors to make it a shared showroom like in the food

126

court. They were all for it, and we had numerous companies willing to go into it with us.

At the last minute, the center backed out and we had to scramble to get into a showroom before the next show. We had talked with the other companies and they were with us until the last minute. We had already signed a contract and committed ourselves. We were only able to bring in about ten companies. They would each pay a commission and a monthly fee. It was not quite enough, but we hoped to bring in more companies. After two years, we had to shut down. In 2000, the bottom seemed to fall out of the wholesale giftware industry. We believed it was because the center had messed up the American Craft Market. They dismantled it, and our regular customers were going elsewhere. January of 2001 was our last show in the showroom. It was fun while it lasted. That was also when I shut down Mae's Place Ceramics. It was all a great experience. The building we showed in, Trade Mart, was the place that President Kennedy was heading to when he was shot. There were pictures around the Mart, showing all the tables set up and ready for the President, along with people standing around with somber looks and expressions.

Cloe and I had a lot in common. We are like sisters and get together whenever we can at the beach where she lives. When she was young, she floated around from home to home, never knowing where she would end up. Her grandparents took care of her after a while. She was an only child, so as an adult, the relationship she had with her mother was not exactly the normal mother-daughter relationship, but what is "normal"? She also had a bad first marriage.

I learned a lot from her. She had common sense and a way of dealing with people that can really make them feel comfortable. It is very easy to talk with her about anything. During shows, we would sit in the hotel just hashing out ideas and making each other laugh.

We still had Wiley for a few years after moving to Waller. We also had Martha, the cat we brought from Katy, with us. Martha just tolerated Wiley, and though he would pester Martha from time to time, he left her alone for the most part. One day, Martha killed the next-door neighbor's rabbit. It had gotten past all eight or so cats in his yard, and Martha claimed the prize. She had hidden it under the deck in back of the house. Wiley went nuts, and one night, he finally dug it out to show us.

About two weeks later, Jeremy came home from the fair with a rabbit named Thumper. I didn't know what to do with it. I talked my neighbor into letting us use the cage from his rabbit to keep it in. I learned that one could box train rabbits. This was new for me. I was afraid of Wiley and Martha getting too close, but it soon became Wiley's pet. Every morning, before going across the street to do his business, he had to run around to Thumper to check on him. I put it in the ceramic shop after a while. Wiley and Thumper became friends. I could soon let it out of the cage and they would chase each other around the shop and lay next to each other. Martha learned to just tolerate it as well.

One day, the shop door was open and Wiley was lying over the threshold watching his rabbit in the back yard. Thumper was following Martha around the right side of the pool. Martha jumped up onto the diving board, and Thumper went underneath it. Just as Martha was jumping down from the diving board, Thumper hopped out and ran into Martha. She turned around and swatted at Thumper. The next thing I knew Wiley was running all out down the left side of the pool and got into Martha's face and growled at her. She just walked off like he was really nothing to be afraid of.

That crazy Thumper would run in circles around us if we were standing outside. He would get a little too close to the chop saw when Dwayne was working on the hot tub decking, so he would push Thumper away. If Wiley saw this, he would get into Dwayne's face, so we had to get rid of Thumper. I found a friend that took him and made him her inside pet. I had never expected to see a Rottweiler and a rabbit as friends.

The Nightmare

Our nightmare started with an innocent friendship between Jeremy and Gill. Jeremy, sixteen years old, and Gill, thirteen. I could see that Gill was starving for the friendship of an older brother-like figure in his life. I didn't know much about him, but was warned to watch him because of possible theft accusations. I watched and let the two play together, because there weren't many children in our neighborhood. They did the normal things that boys did, ride bikes and skateboards, listen to the stereo and just hang out together. Gill's home life was apparently abusive and not a real happy one. He had a younger sister and brother, Skye and Kelly. Skye, eight years old, was always trying to get Jeremy's attention. For six months, when Jeremy would go to their house, Skye would get all giddy, and even told a friend that she wanted Jeremy as her boyfriend, even though he was eight years older. Jeremy and Gill's friendship was innocent enough until one day when I got a visit from the police.

He was being charged with aggravated sexual assault. My legs gave out from under me. I could not believe what I was hearing. Fortunately, Jeremy and Anne were in San Antonio with my brother-in-law and nephew on spring break. I didn't know what to do. The police asked me where he was and said that if he didn't turn himself in by the following Monday, they would put out an APB on him. Terrified, I called my husband and brother-in-law immediately. Jeremy couldn't figure out who could have done this. It was like our lives were in a blur. It wasn't sinking in.

A few weeks prior, while walking our Rottweiler, Beverly confronted him yelling, "You stay away from my daughter or I'll file charges!" He knew that he hadn't done anything, so he shrugged it off at the time, as the ranting of a drug-induced stupor.

I was working in my shop getting my products ready for a wholesale show in Kansas City, MO. I had booked this show months in advance and already loaded the truck. I was scheduled to leave the following day. My partner, Cloe, was such a great friend to lend her shoulder to cry on. Fortunately, I had an aunt and cousin living in Kansas City, so it was a comfort to know that I would have family support there as well.

My husband was so angry. He couldn't believe that a person could be charged without evidence, so Jeremy just had to be guilty. He accused me of not loving my son enough to stay home with him during this time. I had to arrange for a lawyer to take the case before I could get Jeremy back there. After numerous calls to attorneys and the abuse I took over the phone, I was so frustrated by the time I finally found one that I almost couldn't believe that he was sincere. Some of the attorneys laughed when I asked if there could be a set price for services. I cried after I got off the phone. How could they be so cruel? Mr. Barrett seemed to be a more human and caring person than the others. I learned later that maybe I should have paid more for one of those cruel ones. My heart ached with grief over the circumstances, and not knowing where we would come up with the money was a major factor. We borrowed money and cashed in insurance policies and would make payments.

Once I got a lawyer lined up, my nephew drove Jeremy back to town, and I hid him out of the county at Cloe's house just four miles away until the next day when I took Jeremy into the lawyer's office.

Mr. Barrett, the lawyer, told us what to expect, but there is no amount of preparation for what was to come. We hid Jeremy out at my sister's house until he could turn himself into the court the next day. She lived forty-five miles away and I left for Kansas City.

The whole time Dwayne was so emotionally draining for me that I knew for sure that we would have been divorced now if I had stayed. I couldn't get him to believe in Jeremy's innocence. It was better that Jeremy stay with my sister for the remainder of spring break, away from Dwayne.

I cried all of the way to Kansas City. Cloe must have thought I was a blubbering idiot. I just couldn't believe this was happening. I believed my son and nothing anyone could say would change my mind. I wanted to be there by his side, but I had these obligations, and could not afford, especially now, to back out of the show.

My Aunt Betty was so supportive and a rock when I needed one. I would cry myself to sleep and burst into tears at the drop of a hat. It took all I had to muster up the strength to do my job. In the meantime, my sister, Betsy, took care of my son. They went to court and the judge released him on a PR Bond. He spent the rest of the time with her until school started. Anne came home from Annette's and stayed there as well.

Dwayne still would not budge from his determination. I made it back from Kansas City, and the kids started school. Jeremy was immediately taken out of mainstream classes and put into an alternative school. Because of the charge, he was not allowed to be in regular classes.

He was put into a storefront room, on Main St., with about a dozen other children, and two teachers that were really just baby sitters. They couldn't help with much of his work, so I had to fight to get him help with some of his class work. The windows were papered over, so they saw no sunshine and were not allowed a break time to go outside. They couldn't talk to each other. There were no class discussions, and the teachers wouldn't give them enough work to keep them occupied for the full eight hours in class. They weren't allowed to bring in any other material to read, and lunches had to be brought from home. Half of the kids there were about to go insane. Some may have deserved to be there, but nobody deserved that kind of treatment. Children need to stay occupied and need sunshine and exercise. The grades of the kids there ranged from 5th to 12th grades.

I had talked to the school superintendent about letting Jeremy out for a work release program, but because of the charges, he was not allowed to do this, and had to remain in alternative school. I had to fight the teachers to get his work to him, and tutoring was a necessity. Jeremy had been tutoring the others in algebra, but when he needed help in pre-calculus, the head of the math department said he would just tailor his assignments so that Jeremy would not need tutoring. But that wasn't right and I demanded that he send someone down to tutor him. The department head, Mr. Ladden, did it himself. Jeremy was usually done with his work by 10:00, so I would take him out of school the maximum number of days allowed just to give him a break, and to help me in the shop. By the end of the school year, he was about to go nuts. He pleaded with me to not put him back in that school the next year if it went that long.

About the second week before the end of school, Gill was beaten up at school, and Jeremy was blamed for it. It appears that Janie, Jeremy's teacher's daughter, was accused of letting Jeremy talk her into setting up Gill at school. As it turned out, Gill was such a jerk that a couple of the Hispanic kids at school surrounded and threatened him because he was such a bully. Janie was being accused of being one of the head Hispanic leaders of a group. She is Caucasian and can't even speak Spanish. Jeremy had known Janie through Gill because she had been Gill's girlfriend at one time.

We had to hire a private detective; what a waste of money. He didn't and couldn't really talk to anyone there because the locals don't speak to strangers. All he did was take pictures of their trailer, went over the family's statements and point out discrepancies, which I had already done. He sat with the lawyer in the courtroom to help him point out and catch certain things. He did nothing that I didn't do myself. I'll never do that again.

Dwayne finally went with us to the lawyer's office and asked him, "How could Jeremy have been charged with no proof?"

Mr. Barrett asked him if he had ever let Anne have a sleep over. "All it takes is one of them to say that you touched her, and you would be sitting right there where your son is," Mr. Barrett said.

I think that was the pivotal point that changed Dwayne's mind. His attitude finally changed.

Jeremy was upset because Susanna's dad, Cory, made them break up. He felt that was the best thing for her, and I couldn't disagree. Jeremy was going through hell, and they were just too young to weather that storm. Who knew how long it would last?

I have done a lot of praying for patience and guidance. I have always believed that the Lord never gives us more than we can handle, though lately, I feel that I can't handle any more. I just have to accept the support of my friends and family. Without them, I would not have made it this far.

After a while, Skye started more problems, and Jeremy didn't help any by going over to Carl's house, which was in the next block from Skye. Jeremy would go over there to ride with Carl to church on Sundays. Skye and her parents told the DA that he was bothering her and lied about him driving by their house when he was miles away in a different car than they stated. They wanted to put Jeremy in jail, but the judge told him to change his residence and move to Houston.

It was so hard for me to see him leave. He was seventeen at the time and had started home schooling for his senior year. He was also working full time with Dwayne as a glazer. He now had to move into my in-law's house, which was close to work; thank God for small favors. He was also not allowed to go near the only grocery store in our town because Skye sold newspapers there.

I always thought that it was best for children to move out once they were ready and had passed their "rites of passage" so to speak. You know, finish school and hit that point in their life when it is just the right time to leave home. Jeremy was not given that chance. He had no options. We were just fortunate enough to have relatives in Houston.

After a few months went by, Jeremy was at Cloe's, about four miles away in Harris County, working on his car with Dwayne. He then drove, via another route rather than by the store to the house to finish working on his car. In the meantime, Anne and I went to the grocery store. There was Skye sitting on the bench, next to the door, selling newspapers, when Anne went in. I sat in my car and never got out, but had a stare down with Skye. We left, and later in the afternoon, Anne drove back up there and went into the other door so that she wouldn't pass Skye. What mother would leave an eight-year-old at a busy store, by herself, selling newspapers?

We got notice that the DA was going to send down another indictment, so I told Anne not to tell Jeremy since he was to take his SAT the following week. Anne was so mad that Skye was doing this. I told her to not blame Skye because I was sure that it was her mother doing this. They used the same bus stop for school, and Anne wanted to just punch her. I calmed her down and told her to pray that God would touch this family and this would end soon.

The next day Anne handed Skye a book that she had been using in Bible Study. Our neighbor, Susanna, was with Anne when she gave Skye the book. Anne just handed it to her and told her, "I am not thy convector and I hope this book brings you comfort." Anne had highlighted some passages in it while going through Bible study. Skye called her friend Brook, not knowing what to do. I think that she was afraid of what her mother would do. When they got off of the bus that afternoon, Beverly, Skye's mother, and some of her teenage friends were waiting to jump Anne. Fortunately, they didn't do anything. The next day Beverly was coming down the street, so Anne and Susanna went down to the next stop. When the bus reached Skye's stop, Beverly got onto the bus and shouted at Anne to keep her hands off of her daughter or she would file charges on her as well. Someone turned to Anne and told her to look at Skye's forehead. There was a big goose egg bump.

Sure enough, Beverly went to the police and tried to file charges on Anne for assault. The DA told her to drop it and keep her mouth shut about the case.

Not much time passed, and we were called into court again. This time Dwayne went with us. Skye had fabricated a full story about Jeremy going into the store

134

with me and Anne waiting in the car; they were in about five minutes. Then later Jeremy comes back and walks right past her into the store to talk with Carl. We proved to the judge that this did not happen. Instead Anne and I were the only ones that went to the store. I think that by now she was starting to realize that Jeremy was being wronged.

She started asking Dwayne about Jeremy's work and school. I think she could now see, that Jeremy was not a bad kid. However, when they brought up the bus incident, the judge got quite upset with Anne. Because of the passages that were highlighted, the judge couldn't believe that Anne didn't highlight them just for Skye.

She yelled, "I don't know who to throw in jail, you or your brother!" I was really surprised that Anne kept her cool.

The judge kept asking, "How would you feel if someone handed this to you with 'Thou shall not bare false testimony', 'you shall not tell lies', etc."

Anne was trying to explain that she had highlighted these, and all of the others, in bible study, and only thought that the book would comfort Skye and help bring her peace with God and herself. The judge told Jeremy to stay out of Waller County, except to come to court. And Anne was not to ride the school bus anymore. Jeremy couldn't come home for <u>any</u> reason. My heart dropped. I could see all of the future holiday celebrations being very dismal without my family together. Now I had to take Anne to and from school every day. My tax dollars at work. I wondered if I could get a refund.

I was so frustrated. I went to a friend of mine that was a County Sheriff's deputy. I know that the city officer, Pearl Cleveland, usually had holes in her cases. Was there any way to clean this up and hopefully get Pearl Cleveland to do a better job investigating? He advised me that if she did a better job, she might fill it in with better information that could hurt Jeremy. I told him that there was nothing around to hurt him. Unfortunately, things did not get any better. Her husband, Chief Cleveland, tried to solicit our investigator for $50 to obtain information that was supposed to be handed over to us by court order. Unfortunately, the PI's recorder wasn't working, or we could have had a case against the Chief. The State Attorney General's office said that it was too late to try to get it on tape again. Pearl also went to Jeremy's previous teacher and tried to intimidate her not to talk to our investigator. I have learned to hate small towns.

Skye accused him of molesting her while he was at their house on March 5th, and almost every day for the past two years. The Grand Jury handed down 3 indictments. The charges were aggravated sexual assault on Feb 28th and March 5th. Ten months later, they charged him with two more indictments, stating that he performed oral sex on her on January 19th. Jeremy broke his collarbone on February 23rd. It was a physical impossibility for him to have even done anything on two of the indictments, and Gill was with him when it happened.

I think that they remembered this after the fact, and decided to make up this other charge. The January charge is almost as ridiculous. Why would he do anything with ten other people in the trailer house? This family was known to do drugs, both legal and illegal, along with the Sheldon family, whom they hung out with all of the time and were called as witnesses. We believe that these folks got together and concocted this whole story to cover their butts after something happened at home. Beverly was an incest survivor that never got help. We think that a motive she may have had was to get money from us, but we just didn't understand any of this.

Over the next few years, we endured the nightmare and horror of an unbalanced judicial system. When they say that justice is blind, they weren't kidding; blind to the facts that surround a case that cannot be introduced into a trial.

Sometimes life deals you such a raw deal. I have to keep telling myself that the Lord never gives us more than we can handle. It's tough sometimes. I have to stop and pray for the strength and guidance we all need. As long as I have faith that it will work out, it does. The Lord works through my friends and family. With their support and love, we made it through this.

I remembered so many years ago, when my faith was shaken and my life fell apart, I waited too long to pray for the guidance I needed. Once I did though, I was able to find the strength again and pull myself out of that hole.

Well, the devil was trying again and I wouldn't let him take over again. I prayed all of the time for my family. I wished that Dwayne and Jeremy would put faith in the Lord. I knew that if Dwayne would truly believe, the Lord would show him the way to a calmer existence.

We will always wonder why things happen, but the best we can do is put faith in the Lord, and the answer will come in His time, not ours. But the answers do come. It may not be the answer we were looking for, but God knows best. I just couldn't figure out why the Batts were doing this to my family. Maybe they saw that we moved a business into Waller and thought that we had money.

We went to trial the first time, where two of the five charges were dropped, and he was found not guilty on two charges. On the January charge, the jury was deadlocked. One juror refused to accept the reasonable doubt factor. Duh, they found that she was lying on the February and March charges; there is the doubt factor. We found out later that a juror talked to someone at lunch. Maybe it was the same one that was holding out. If the lawyer had been more persistent with his questioning, and hit on some of the things I told him too, we might not have been facing another trial. We had eleven postponements between the trials. I wondered if this nightmare would ever end.

Skye had gone through chemotherapy when she was a baby and developed earlier than normal. She started puberty at the age of seven. Her hormones were raging, and she didn't know how to handle them. Her mother stayed messed up on drugs or something, according to Jeremy and others. Her parents were physically and mentally abusive to the children. Though we could not prove any of this, I believed it to be true.

I see how the rich can get away with so much. For every expert, there are experts to counter. For every opinion, there is an opposite opinion. All of this costs money. Money that we don't have.

Tim was no help at all. I called him when this first started to see if he could help, even a little. That was a waste of time. I asked him to at least call Jeremy and offer his support. That never happened. I felt so bad for Jeremy that his own father wouldn't support him. Anytime I talked with Tim, all he would say was, "Is he in jail yet?" I wanted to strangle him right through the phone. I should have known that insensitive creep would act that way.

Anne calls him "the donor". Dwayne is their father, and they both openly admitted it is so. I don't think that Dwayne could love them any more if they were his own. In spite of all the hardships we have endured through the trials, we have been a family united.

We are years down the road now, 2003, and there have been so many trials and tribulations. Seven years have passed, and Jeremy has a wife and son, but things have not changed. He lost the appeals process and his probation has started over this year. Now all of the restrictions are upon him and all of us.

After the second trial, Skye admitted to a mutual acquaintance that her brother had molested her. We had suspected this because as soon as the charges were brought against Jeremy, the Batts moved Gill to his grandparents. The day before the first trial, he tried to commit suicide. None of this could be brought up at the trial, because they said it wasn't relevant.

He had to go through different phases of his psychiatric probation. The first one, he said, would last for a year and a half. In this phase, he was not allowed to carry a picture of his son in his wallet, bathe him or go anywhere there are children under the age of seventeen, including the family Christmas party. We couldn't even do trick-or-treaters. I missed the smiling faces of the children at my door on Halloween.

During this whole ordeal, we had to live our lives. I encouraged Jeremy to go to college. He was working with Dwayne and living in Houston. First, he was with my in-laws, but then they both quit that glass company and went back to Amarillo, so Jeremy moved in with Mother in Annette's townhouse. We looked at several colleges to see what they had to offer in the graphic design programs. The Art Institute of Houston offered the best program for him. Students get to work constantly on their portfolio and earn an Associate's degree. Since he was homeschooled his senior year, we weren't sure that would be accepted, but I met with the dean and he was all for it. He said that his wife homeschooled his children.

Jeremy excelled at the design work. He worked full time and went to school at night. Dwayne and Gordan were not too happy when he couldn't work overtime. I tried to explain to Dwayne that he has to get on with his life, regardless of what the outcome would be. Dwayne figured that he should just work and put away the money, and then when this was all over, he could go to college. I don't think that he would have gone later. Procrastination is too easy to get by with when there is nobody around to encourage you.

My mother moved out and Jeremy stayed in the townhouse and rented it from Annette. He took in a roommate to share the cost, but then the roommate moved his estranged wife and kids in without consulting Annette, and they really messed the place up. The kids drew on just about every wall in the place. Jeremy started seeing Dora, and she moved in as well.

Dora

We weren't too sure about Dora. She had been in a bad situation with her mother's boyfriend, and Jeremy felt that he had to rescue her. They were on and off for a while, but they moved to another apartment together. I had hoped he would stay on his own for a while, but what do I know?

One day, I was driving into the parking lot when she stopped me and cried on my shoulder about loving him so much, and he was being unfair. He had kicked her out of the apartment. I tried to tell her that maybe they both needed to be on their own for a while in order to understand one's self, and if it was meant to be, they would get back together.

She fooled around on him several times, and maybe this was one of them. I don't understand why guys marry someone that fools around on them, expecting that they won't do it again.

They married anyway, and looking back at the pictures, neither one really looked very happy. It should have been a red flag, but parents can only advise and hope their children consider the advice. All we can do is support them in their decisions and prop them up when they fall.

Dora soon got pregnant. She worked fairly close to where I was working at the time, so there were times that I would take her to her doctor in the Medical Center if she was having a problem with the pregnancy. We seemed to get along pretty well. When she had the baby, our grandson, Daniel (Dan for short), everything changed. She became the devil incarnate.

The day after Dan was born, I went to the hospital to see him. I felt so bad for him. He was lying there with tubes and wires attached to his tiny body. I held him for about an hour, just singing and talking to him. I hoped a little bonding would be good for him. We got our first grandson, and life was good. He soon got out of the hospital and went home.

Jeremy was in the middle of his appeal and had a fractured ankle, so he was able to stay at home and take care of Dan. We met a few times for lunch. Dan seemed to be so aware of his surroundings. I loved being able to spend time with them.

After a time, they separated again, and Jeremy moved home with us. Not long after, they got back together and they all moved in with us. But them living with us had not been all roses. I was able to stay home and take care of Dan. I loved being able to do this.

He was about one-year old and not talking at all. It was hard to communicate with him, so I started teaching him sign language. I didn't do the full signing, just some simple gestures so we could communicate. Dora said that this was hindering his speaking and she refused to communicate with him this way. Everyone would be more frustrated, not knowing what he was wanting.

I never put stuff out of reach with my kids and refused to do it with Dan. Of course, I would never leave anything out that could hurt them, but they learned not to bother things. Dan learned what he could play with and not. If Dwayne and I went out of town for the weekend, we would come back to having to put everything back in place. They refused to work with me and teach him what was not to be touched. Instead, they would just push everything out of reach.

Despite all this, after about another three months or so he started talking. I guess he felt it was easier to talk than to do sign language. He was a pretty smart child and such a delight to be with. He didn't misbehave when we went out to dinner or on outings.

No matter what I did, it was the wrong thing in Dora's eyes. I know how it is when you are staying with someone else. They don't always want you in their territory, like the kitchen. One night I was making dinner and mentioned to her that she was welcome to use the kitchen anytime she wanted. She told Jeremy that I was telling her to get off her lazy fanny and cook.

I decided to get pictures of Dan by a professional at Sears. I thought that Jeremy and Dora would like to have a set of pictures of him for Christmas, so I took him for a photo shoot. We had fun and took lots of pictures. I had a cute one of him on my back, among others with him and me together, as well as the others by himself. I purchased the USB drive with all the pictures and had a few blown up to give to Jeremy and Dora. One day, Jeremy had to borrow my laptop and Dora saw the one of Dan sitting on my back and flipped out. I had them rotating in the background with other pictures I liked. I told them what I had done and showed them the others, but she thought that it was weird that I would take pictures of just Dan and me. She refused to accept the fact that grandparents take pictures with their grandchildren all the time.

There was no pleasing her. Only when she got her way was she happy. I really don't even think that she could ever be happy.

The straw broke the camel's back finally. Dora had stabbed us in the back for the last time by not letting Dan come in and say hello to his grandpa. She did this often and was cold to us on a constant basis. She didn't realize just what she was doing to everyone involved or she just didn't care. It was like she had blinders on and nobody could tell her differently. She wouldn't take advice from anyone. Instead, she would go in the opposite direction, no matter what you said. Maybe we should have been using reverse psychology on her like a child. I guess it was a character flaw and there was nothing that could fix it. I feel bad for Jeremy and Dan. She just didn't realize that Dan was going to run from her every chance he got and as soon as he could. On the other hand, if she kept him from us and poisoned his mind about us, he would grow to hate us until he learned differently. Hopefully it wouldn't be too late for him to know that we love him. I feared that he would turn out to despise her and everyone around him as she does, which would rot his insides out and make him callous like her. It was time for tough love and for them to move out.

They needed a place of their own to be a family. Unfortunately, it wouldn't be a happy family, ever. But they needed to be on their own without our interference, and though it wouldn't improve, I knew that they would have to find their path their own way. The best we could do is to let Jeremy and Dan know that we are here for them and love them. Tough love is hard for all concerned.

Over time we learned how bad things can really get with a manipulator hard at work. Dora would threaten us, and Jeremy, all the time, using Jeremy's convictions against him and us. She would use Dan as a tool to get what she wanted instead of what was best for him. Our life had been turned upside down because of this woman. I was to pick up Dan because I was a chaperone. She would not give an inch to let us pick him up from school or when there was a special event. It always had to be right at the time specified.

As Dan got older and Jeremy moved on, we'd hoped that they would have been able to work things out with Dan as their first priority. Dora had no part of that. She still used him as a weapon against anything and anyone that Dan loved. She acted like Dan only had so much love and she wanted it all. She didn't understand or couldn't comprehend that the more people that loved Dan, the better person he would become. She was jealous of any love he gave to anyone else.

Well, the crap hit the fan again. One day, Dora comes by unexpectedly to pick up her stuff in the warehouse. Jeremy was letting her, but she started taking his stuff too, so he asked her to leave and she wouldn't, of course. After several urging attempts, Jeremy started to come for me in the house, but she threatened to break everything in sight. She started getting hysterical, so Jeremy grabbed her from behind to get her out of the shop, but she started thrashing around and he let her go. He finally got her out, closed the roll up door, and then she bit him in the chest. She fell backwards on the cobblestone crying when Jeremy pushed her away. In the meantime, I'm trying to keep Dan occupied in the house so he doesn't have to witness their nonsense. I heard him yell," MOM!" in an outcry of pain. I rushed to the door finding Dora on the ground crying, and Jeremy flustered as he showed me his chest where she bit him, after I asked what had happened. I had Dan in my arms by then and took him back into the house.

Jeremy helped her get up and into a chair. Soon she was in her car and yelling at Jeremy. I called Cory from next door to come and get Dan away from here for the moment. Dora was threatening to call the police and have Jeremy arrested, so I called them. Officer Martin came and took statements and pictures. Nobody wanted anyone to get arrested, but I was tired of all the BS and wanted this documented. They both got tickets for Domestic Abuse, which carried a Class C Misdemeanor. They both had to see Judge Becker. Jeremy was worried about his probation, but I thought he would be all right.

While the police were at the house, she demanded that I return Dan to her. She was going to take him home. I refused, saying that it was Jeremy's weekend, and she stated that there were no legal papers proclaiming this. She also told the police that she had given Jeremy the divorce papers and he hadn't signed them. Jeremy had no divorce papers, but did have the court papers declaring the legal visitation.

Over a period of time, we grew to wish this nightmare was over and we didn't have to deal with Dora anymore. However, as long as Dan was with her, she would be in the picture. I was supposed to be the one to pick him up, but after a while, she moved to the northeast corner of Harris County, and started letting Jeremy pick him up without a chaperone. She still pulls stunts that would inconvenience Jeremy and his family. The harassment won't end until Dan is out on his own. I feel so bad for Dan, that he has not been allowed to really enjoy his childhood. Having to babysit his sisters all the time just shows how lazy and selfish Dora really is.

Star International

After I closed down my shop in 2001, I got a job with a company that imported beaded fringes and trims. They wanted me to get more production out of their warehouse staff. Some of them didn't speak English, so I had to have someone translate for me. After a short period of time, I had finally had enough and told one of the guys that I was not going to walk all the way over to the other side of the warehouse just to get someone to translate for him. I told him to do something, and I even showed him the way I wanted it done. He knew what I was saying. After that the owner, Phil, pulled me into the office and told me that maybe it wasn't the best time to try to get these people in the warehouse to cooperate. He moved me into the office instead.

I started putting together products for the wholesale shows and buyers. I organized shows in New York and Seattle at the same time and would travel to all the shows. I liked doing this on someone else's dime for once. It didn't take long to set up the space for the shows, so I went site-seeing. I really enjoyed this job, but got a bit tired of living out of a suitcase in New York for five or six days, home for one, then on to Las Vegas for another four. Phil also had me overseeing renovations and plumbing problems.

I had read the book "Fish" by Harry Paul, John Christensen and Stephen C. Lundin. It is a self-help book that really hit home. I had finally found something that fit my personality. I wanted to implement it at work, but Phil would never read his copy. After a while, I started putting up signs around the office and warehouse like, "ATTITUDE...what attitude do you bring in to work with you?" Then another one was, "Make someone's day, you'll both feel better." I finally quit because Phil started accusing me of stealing and thought I was working another job. I just wanted the respect I deserved and tried to help make it a better place to work.

Attitudes did seem to improve, and on my last day, the warehouse crew asked if it was me putting up the signs. They laughed. They learned to respect me more by then. We had become friends, as well.

September 11, 2001, I had just awakened and turned on the television, and what do I see but the World Trade Center on fire. It was on the BBC, so I turned to a local channel, thinking this was some cruel movie. It was real. I couldn't believe my ears and what I was seeing on the television. I called my sisters and husband to let them know what was going on. Their reactions were like mine. This just couldn't be happening to us on our soil.

No one could stop watching history unfold on the television. I ran into the living room and started recording it on the VCR. That moment would change our lives forever. We would no longer feel totally safe on public transportation, especially airplanes. We would now and forever, think twice about what could happen and where. Our false sense of security had been forever shaken.

There are United States flags everywhere and churches are reporting record attendance. We have come together as one nation. I hope and pray for our country to heal and find hope for a brighter future.

Adoption

I was in New York in January, just after the 911 attacks. I was doing the tourist thing and went to ground zero. It was an ominous feeling. The grates that spanned the perimeter were not too easy to see through, but I was able to see the excavation in progress. Almost all of the rubble was taken out by then and one could see the damage below ground level. There were people milling around with their conspiracy theories. The pictures of the day of the attack were around everywhere. I visited the church where the cemetery stones had been under four feet of ash. It was a small cemetery next to a small church, but the love of the community was evident. The cleanup was well done and everything was back to normal, if you could call it that.

I walked all over the southern side of Manhattan. I was not impressed with anything about the town, except for the giant video screens in Times Square. I had met up with a friend from the Dallas World Trade Center. Joseph was from New Jersey. He took me around town and showed me some of the sights. He took me to the fire station where the town decided to make a memorial for the lost firemen, but their station didn't lose anyone in the World Trade Center.

I had known Joseph from my days at the Dallas World Trade Center wholesale shows. He sold dried flowers and had his booth across from ours at the flower show. He was a really nice guy and fun to joke around with. I kept telling him that he needed to move to Texas, but he was adamant about living in New York. He loves the city and wants to move there one day. As we were walking around town, we came across Times Square, and big as life there is a steak house on the corner in the middle of it all. The name of the restaurant was "Texas Steakhouse". I told him, "see, even New York likes Texas and can't do without it in some way." We both just laughed.

While I was in New York, Anne and Dwayne discussed her adoption. She had always wanted him to adopt her, so finally they decided to go through with it. When the time came for the adoption to go to court, the judge thought it was fun to have such an old child as the adoptee. He asked Dwayne if he was taking her out for ice cream after this. She was now officially Dwayne's daughter. She even had Tim's name taken off her birth certificate.

Getting the Harleys

In January of 2012, Dwayne called me, on his way home, to tell me that he had purchased a Harley Davidson. He had been looking at bikes for the past year because when he was a teenager, he was at a friend's house when he had accidentally knocked over the friend's new Harley. Why this would pique his interest so high, I'll never know. I guess it is a male thing.

The following day, he brought home the new toy and parked it right next to my ceramic kiln. I had to move it to get into my kiln. I have never been on a motorcycle by myself before, so I tried to back it out and turn it around. Mistake. I felt it falling so I let it down as carefully as I could. I had to call a friend from next door over to move it for me. It had a few scratches on it, and I was devastated. I dreaded telling Dwayne when he got home. It wasn't as bad as I thought. He told me, "Remember when I knocked over my friend's Harley? Payback was coming."

We went for our first ride together riding tandem. It was fun. He told me that either I needed to learn to ride, and we get another bike, or I might become a motorcycle widow come spring. So we decided to take the classes together. Just before the class, we bought a Suzuki for me since I had no experience and it was cheaper than the Harley.

I practiced around town and decided to take it to the funeral home parking lot to practice my turns. Wouldn't you know it? I got the bike stuck in the row of hedges. Then on the way home, it fell over when I stopped at a stop sign. I was fed up with it and decided to park it until I took the classes. Dwayne asked me if I was ready to give it up completely. I told him, "No, I'm not going to let it beat me."

We took the classes and I learned a lot. I highly recommend it for anyone, experienced or not. Dwayne told me that, even though he had ridden since he was a teen, he still learned some, and it also helped him to remember what to look for when driving. We decided to take our first trip to Colorado and Wyoming.

When driving in the Colorado Mountains, and the signs say ten miles an hour, they mean it. Riding motorcycles in the mountains is not for the sightseer. One must pay attention to the road. I think we both had a few close calls. I am glad we had decided to purchase some headphones. We could communicate while driving.

There is a natural freedom about riding around on motorcycles. This was something we could do together. While on our trips, we would make camp and go ride around the area for a few hours, then repeat the following day. Major pitfalls are the wasps flying up your sleeve while riding. It is not a good feeling having the thing stinging you while trying to find a place to pull over.

After about two years, I was ready to upgrade, so we purchased a used Harley for me. I was now riding with the big boys. Previously, I felt a little out of place. When we would ride, I would sometimes park in the far parking lot away from the other Harleys. Sometimes there are prejudices about the non-Harley crowd. I was envious. Now I would have my own, but still needed more experience because it was still falling over. We finally took the advanced classes, and it hasn't fallen since.

On my birthday, Jeremy got me some Air Force placards for my bike and Dwayne got me new, louder, pipes. I no longer have pipe envy.

We would take many rides together around our area to see the bluebonnets and some of our wonderful countryside.

One day we decided to ride up to Austin for the Rot Rally. We decided to ride on up to our property near Marble Falls. By the time we got within an hour of home, our butts were so sore we had to stop. I decided not to take any long trips like that again. I would be more than happy to trailer them for long trips.

Back to School

I decided to go back to school and get my Medical Coding Certification. I had done this while working at the home health care agency back in 1983, when the CPT and ICD9 were only about the size of a small paperback book and half an inch thick. Now they were the size of text books, and two to three inches thick. I went to Houston Community College (HCC) and took some classes; eventually I passed the state exam and got my certification.

I found a job with a cardiologist in the Medical Center with a cardiology group. Cardiology is the most difficult to code. I took the Metro Ride to and from, which was two hours each way. The pay was not too bad, but what I had to put up with was not. The other coder and I worked in a small area with two other girls, and when the whole office would come back to our area to chat. They would get too loud, and I couldn't talk to the insurance companies very easily because they would make my mic key off at the wrong time for the automated services on the other end. I finally decided that was enough.

During this three-month period, Betsy did an internship at the Medical Center for MRI, so we rode the bus and train together. She was needing a month of an internship, but in the midst of this, Annette ended up in the hospital in New Braunfels with a major problem with her colon or intestines. Since Betsy was between jobs, she went over there to be with Annette and help her out. She wound up finding a job and moving there.

After just three months, I couldn't take it anymore and quit my job. I would look for something a little closer to home, and hopefully, not so crazy.

It didn't take too long and I found a job in Katy with a medical group of nine practitioners. We had a pulmonologist, gastroenterologist, OB/GYN, and internal medicine. I was hired to fill a position created for patient collections and insurance billing.

151

The people I worked with were terrific and it was a big enough office that everyone could spread out. Most everyone was in an office of their own or with one other person. I shared mine with one other woman. One of the physician assistants was in the Air Force Reserves. She and I had a little camaraderie going on. On one of her visits somewhere, she brought me back a glass crystal with the USAF emblem on it for my desk.

Dan was in a daycare not too far from my office, so when he got sick, I was able to bring him into work with me and see one of my doctors. Since Dwayne or I had to pick Dan up at daycare, we really liked the location and he was learning a lot there.

One day, Dora asked me if we could help her out on her daycare bill, which she had fallen behind $750. I told her no, but I would discuss it with Dwayne. We just didn't want him leaving this daycare though, so Dwayne paid $1100 on her bill and told them not to tell her about the overage because she would fall behind again. This seemed to be a pattern for her to hop around to different daycare centers owing them money.

I got a call later in the week that Dan was ill and they were unable to get a hold of Dora; she was having surgery. I called Jeremy to see what the matter was. He told me that she was having breast implants done. I was furious. I swore that we would not give her one more dime. Her dad, Matt, knew about the surgery and refused to help her, so she cut him out of Dan's life. We did not find out about this until about three months down the road.

Dan was upset about not being able to talk to, or see, Matt. When he was not with us, she let him go with Matt for the weekends. This was not fair, so we let him call Matt from our house, and he came out to our place to visit him.

One day after I picked Dan up, he told me that his mama said that I was crazy. I turned around and told him that was right.

"Isn't it better to be a little crazy than uptight?" He just laughed. I know that Dora was just being facetious, but I had to turn it around. He was only about four years old, so I always tried to not say anything bad about Dora in front of Dan, after all, she was his mom. I am sure that she said all kinds of bad stuff about us.

I had co-signed on a loan for her to get a new car. I didn't want her driving around in a piece of crap with Dan riding with her. At that point, she and Jeremy were getting back together. She started falling behind on payments from time to time and I had to pay it so it wouldn't go on my record. One time we found out that she had no valid license and no insurance. Dwayne and I went to her apartment, took out the car seat and Dan's coat, and as I was driving off, he went upstairs to tell her. He told her that he would come get her and Dan the next day, so she would not miss work. She was really mad and said that she would stand in front of him so he couldn't leave. He just held up the car seat and said that it was gone. He told her to get her affairs in order because we could not afford to let anything happen that would cause someone to sue us. The car smelled so bad. It reminded me of driving the Domino's car with stale odors. The following day there was a fax at his office for proof of insurance and he verified the license with a police officer he knew. He gave her the car back.

Anne & Lorenzo

When Anne graduated high school, she started going to school at night with the Art Institute of Houston for Culinary Arts and working at a local restaurant. Not too long after, she went to work with a construction company at Prairie View A&M, still going to school. She really liked the classes and instructors. She really fit into this vocation. She also liked working with the construction company.

Soon, she became friends with one of the Houston executives. Lorenzo was older and she wasn't sure if she should go out with him. She asked me if I thought it was proper to ask Lorenzo out for drinks. I told her that it didn't matter what the age difference, as long as she felt comfortable with him. They hit it off, and after a long dating period, I was concerned about what they really wanted, and if Lorenzo just wanted arm candy or a partner. I knew that Anne wanted kids, and I was not sure if Lorenzo, with four kids, wanted more. They discussed it and split up for two weeks. They discussed all the issues and got back together. They decided to get married in a small ceremony at their favorite restaurant. I joked with her about instantly becoming a grandma. She fired back with, "That makes you a great-grandma." Oops. We could not have picked a better husband for her. Lorenzo was almost thirty years her senior, but they were great together.

Anne never finished her degree in culinary arts because they only offered the last class during the daytime. She also needed to do an internship, and there were no real restaurants in our area where she could do this. She has since achieved a Bachelor's degree from WGU in Business Management.

Irvin

My step-dad Irvin had fallen and had a brain bleed. He had developed dementia and his wife, Dawn, was really having a hard time with him. I decided that I would quit working and help her out, letting Irvin stay with us a few days a week to give her a break.

I had been working with the medical group for a year and a half, and it seemed that every time someone would do something wrong, the manager would blast us with an email for everyone to be reprimanded. She would complain about behavior and still not confront that person about it. I had made arrangements before I came to work that I would take two weeks off around Labor Day for vacation, and it became a fight whenever the time came.

The job they hired me to do was to collect money from the patients. When I would finally get some of the patients to pay on a regular basis, they would go to the doctor and claim to be broke and the physician would want me to write it off. I finally told the manager that I was spinning my wheels. Why did they hire me if they were going to constantly write them off? I might as well just quit and do some good for my family.

Irvin went back into the hospital for another fall and brain bleed, even worse with the brain pushing off to one side. He was in ICU for a few days and eventually moved to a hospice care facility. He never regained consciousness. A few days before I quit, Dawn asked me about taking Irvin off life support. I agreed, and now it was just a waiting game. My last day at work they threw me a good-bye party and I got the phone call that Irvin was on his way out. I went to the hospice care facility and we both said our good-byes.

Irvin had been a very important part of my life. We had gone thru a lot together. It wasn't always easy, but we gained respect for each other. I did a lot of praying through life, and now I prayed for God to accept him and take him out of his pain.

My quitting must have been a God thing. I didn't know what He had planned for me, but I would soon find out. Annette needed my help more. She eventually succumbed to the cancer. It had spread to the colon. After she died, there was an argument with the four executrices, and one of her "friends" came and cleaned out the safe with the cash, coin and stamp collections and silver service. They were not getting along, and everyone was out for themselves. One of them, Patty, backed out when it got crazy. She and I looked after Herman. He had sold his house and put the cash in Patty's safe deposit box.

Maggie's husband finally came out of the woodwork. We couldn't find him before, but when he found out that Maggie was gone, he came in to claim everything. The judge deemed the wills invalid and gave him everything. He couldn't get any of the stuff that had been in the safe. Maggie's other friend had essentially stolen it all. Willard showed up with his girlfriend and a motor home and cleaned out the house. He gave me Maggie's pistol. He said in court that he would help Herman get settled somewhere after he sold the house. Willard looked just like my first foster dad, Mr. Deardan, so it was hard seeing Willard being the way he was.

The pipes froze and broke, so I had to get Herman out of there. I had been in the process of getting him an apartment in Waller so he would be closer to me. I moved him in with us for a week or two until the apartment was ready. My friend, Laura, and I took care of him under the provider services. We split days during the week. This made it easier for both of us. I was back in school at HCC to earn an Associate's degree in Real Estate.

Mira had worked at Tenneco, overseeing many Right-of-Way Agents, so she thought that she could get my foot in the door with someone she knew. I had to get my Real Estate License first. I was able to get into the Real Estate program at HCC, under the Hazelwood Act.

Herman was sort of a simpleton. He never held a sophisticated job. He had been in the reserves for a short period of time and took janitorial or maintenance jobs for most of his life. He was friendly to everyone and had simple needs. He watched the television most of the day. We would get him outside to walk at least once a day. He had a dog named Dixie. She was a red healer and his constant companion.

Herman was easy to care for and didn't demand anything. I think he was just happy to have his dog, a place to live, and someone to talk to. Laura and I switched off with his care, so neither of us would be tied down completely.

In 2012, Herman died while in the hospital. It was a sad day for Laura and me. I had to make the decision to stop life support. I hated doing this, but he was brain dead and not breathing on his own. It was very sad that he didn't have any more friends besides Patty, Laura, Ruby and me. He is missed.

Maggie Lurvey

My friend, Maggie, couldn't get insurance because she had lupus at one time. She owned a flower shop and could barely afford to see a doctor. She finally went for a pap smear and they found cancerous cells. She needed to have a hysterectomy. She couldn't afford this either. I talked with one of my GYN doctors and she agreed to do it, if the hospital would approve her coming in. Maggie felt that there was something wrong with her colon as well, so I got our gastroenterologist to agree to do a colonoscopy while she was in the hospital.

She had filed for Medicare, but was denied and just needed a letter from the Waller County courthouse to that effect. They were dragging their feet, so she was having problems proving indigent status. Memorial Hermann told me that they were a "for profit" hospital, and she could pay $9000 cash. They would not let her come under indigent status without the letter saying she had been denied Medicare. Maggie finally got the letter. The hospital finally approved her for the hysterectomy, but not the colonoscopy. They said that it was not medically necessary.

After the hysterectomy, the doctor referred her to an oncologist. They finally got her into MD Anderson's program. Eventually I started taking her to her chemo treatments and helped her as best I could around the shop/house. She lived in the house where she worked.
During all of this, our friend Herman had gone into the hospital. He was 82 years old and his house was in deplorable shape with no working hot water, holes in the floor and a horrible smell, from too many animals and just not taking care of himself. Maggie moved him in with her when he got out of the hospital. He had no family and no other friends, so we got him on provider services to help him out. This would help alleviate some of the work Maggie had to do for him.

Maggie had been married to a man named Willard, after only knowing him a few weeks. After three months, he took off with her money and a new van he had convinced her to buy. He made shabby sheik furniture and sold it at craft shows around the area. She wanted a divorce, but refused to sign the papers until he paid her back the money he had taken. This had been going on for three years. She found out that he wanted to marry someone else and had given her a really expensive ring, so she was out for blood. She signed a will that just stated that she didn't want her husband to get anything and didn't name anyone to get her estate. I tried to talk her into doing a legal will. She did another one that I hadn't seen that named four executrices. Neither one was legal.

Steve

A friend from the Methodist church was in his late eighties; his wife had died, so he was lonely. He would call me from time to time, so one day I went to his house for drinks. He lived in a large two-story house with no air conditioning. It was a mess, with cob webs all over and in bulk, a stack of mail, and miscellaneous papers piled high on his dining room table. I asked him if he wanted me to help him get his house cleaned up. He kept talking about how he was dizzy and wanted to see another doctor. I suggested that he see a doctor I knew. I also got him to get his air conditioning fixed. I fixed a plumbing leak and vacuumed his house.

I was taking Steve to see the doctor for a follow-up visit. When we got there, the nurse took us into another room and told us that his daughter had called and cancelled his appointment. She suggested I back off from helping him.

Steve's daughter was bringing a suit against me for trying to kill him and take his money. Steve kept calling me and didn't understand that I couldn't talk or see him anymore. She had a restraining order against me. I was just trying to help out an old friend. I didn't eat or sleep well for the next few months. Thank goodness, I had taken pictures of the condition of things before I started cleaning. I had to get character testimonials from friends to take to the judge. It was like going to one's own funeral. The things that my friends were saying were a little surprising. It was all so nice, and it was very humbling. We finally had a meeting with a mediator and explained to him what all had transpired. Just after this, Steve had a heart attack, went into the hospital and fell. He had broken a hip. He finally came home under hospice. His family was blaming me for his condition. After this, Dwayne told me that it would be better if I stopped helping everyone else and just help out family.

Bert

We got a call from Sadie, Dwayne's stepmom. She said that Bert had overdosed on Tylenol, was in the hospital and not coming back home. We had to come get him. He had cancer the year before and he was depressed. I figured that we could handle him. Dwayne met him in 1983 for the first time since he was a little boy. We had visited him a few times in North Carolina when we would go up to visit with his grandparents.

This was a major ordeal. Bert had not done anything on his own, like cook, pay bills, or organize his life. When he got down here, we moved him in with us until I could get him settled in a place of his own. I helped him get his Medicare, Social Security, banking, and Texas identification straightened out. I set him up with a good doctor and eventually a small house to rent. Not long after he moved into the house, his sister in North Carolina died.

He didn't want to move to Texas, and so this was a blow. He hadn't gotten to see his sister before he left, and now she was dead. He was so mad. I had never seen anyone so mad that they could kill someone until Bert. I have no doubt, that if his wife or step-son had been standing in front of him at that moment, he would have killed them with his bare hands.

Bert was my father-in-law and I wanted to welcome him into our lives, but the situation went south. One-night Dwayne called to tell me to not answer the phone if Bert called or let him into the house if he wasn't there. I figured something bad had happened. This man who we opened our house and hearts to had declared war on my family. He told Dwayne that he should divorce me and move on. I have known my husband for over forty years, and this man only a few months. He wanted to tear apart my family.

We invited him to family gatherings and he declined. Soon he did not want anything to do with us. It was a small town and I kept running into him and his lady friend, whom I had no use for either.

I felt bad that Dwayne couldn't have a relationship with his dad after all this time. Bert had fallen while on a trip to Corpus with Dwayne. He had a major brain bleed and almost died. He was transferred to San Antonio, unconscious. Dwayne went there to be with him, and I joined him a few days later. We stayed with my sister, Betsy, in New Braunfels. We went to the hospital every day. Dwayne was diligent about staying by his side and making sure that the doctors were doing everything possible. I went with him for several days until Bert regained consciousness. After this, I figured it would be better if I weren't around. Dwayne told me that Bert berated him the whole time. He had more stamina than I would have. I certainly would not have put up with it.

While he was still in the hospital, about to be released to rehab, Dwayne wanted me to get Bert's house cleaned up and yard mowed. I hired someone to do both, and I did ten loads of laundry. When Bert came home, he got mad and changed the lock on the door since I had been in his house. We stopped talking to Bert again.

I feel bad that Dwayne can't have a loving relationship with his dad. He tried so hard to make him part of our family, to no avail.

Jeremy & Debbie

Jeremy found a girl that really loved him. Debbie had a son about Dan's age, and was a refugee from Louisiana and Katrina. She moved here with her parents, brothers, and son. They were all a very nice family. I was so happy for Jeremy. We all loved Debbie and her son, Schroeder. They lived in the house that Dora and her husband had purchased. I knew it would not be a very good idea, but it was Jeremy's only chance at the moment, considering his conviction. It had been a problem any time Jeremy wanted to move. The apartments would do a background check, and he would not be able to rent.

They lived there for a couple of years and moved into my step-dad's house. Dawn was moving to California to be with her son, Mike, and his family. They lived there for a year before buying their first house.

Debbie had taken classes online and earned her Bachelor's degree in Biology. She wanted to become a teacher. In the meantime, she got pregnant with our granddaughter, Elizabeth. Giving birth to Elizabeth was a very traumatic ordeal for both of them. She was born at almost ten pounds, and she had her natural. Both were in ICU for four days before she could go see Elizabeth in NICU.

Elizabeth is the apple of her daddy's eye. It is so nice to see them all so happy. I truly believe that God blessed them with each other. They both had bad experiences with their previous relationships, not to mention, Katrina, for Debbie. They were a very happy family.

Dwayne finally had a granddaughter that he could dote after. The saying goes that grandchildren are a parent's best revenge. This is true.

He had a four-wheel drive Jeep to take his family camping and four wheeling. It was great to see them enjoying themselves like they do, getting back to nature. We took our vehicles to the beach also and played in the soft sand. I can't explain the feeling of doing this, except that it is like beating nature just a little.

My aspirations were to take Jeremy and his family back to Guam to show them where he was born. He has a pride in being born there, maybe a bit more than people born in another state because of the mystique of it. It really is a beautiful island with their culture. I hope that it has not changed much with the Japanese taking over much of it. When I was there, the Japanese came to the island because it was close, and I am guessing that it is cheaper than going someplace else. They stayed in Japanese-owned hotels and shopped at only the Japanese-owned shops, therefore most of the money went back to Japan.

Mary Kay

Anne started a new home-based job with Mary Kay. She would call me with such enthusiasm that I would become interested. She told me of what a great faith-based company this was and all the directors were terrific. She wanted me to get into it. I don't wear make-up, so I was really not interested in selling it. I was really happy for her that she found something to keep her upbeat.

One night I agreed to go with her to a meeting with the directors in her unit. I enjoyed hearing their "Me" stories. This is a story of why one gets into selling Mary Kay and becomes a consultant. They start and end every meeting with a prayer. How many companies do that?

One of the directors' "Me" story really hit home. She had been in an abusive relationship. She told us how she got into Mary Kay and found her purpose. It was so uplifting.

I still stuck to my guns about not wearing make-up, but by the end of the meeting, I grew to understand that it was not all about make-up, but skin care. They really focus on taking care of one's skin. The cosmetics are just the frosting on the cake. I signed up that night.

This would be an adventure for Anne and me to share. We went to our first seminar in Dallas. It was loud, fun, and a learning experience. We saw how so many women and some men achieved their goals of becoming directors and earning the pink Cadillac. It really is a great company to work for. I've sold Tupperware, Amway, Trichem liquid embroidery, and Oxyfresh products. This is not to say that the other products were not as good. They are all great products. Of all the home-based businesses, Mary Kay is by far the most exciting, and allows for more of a profit and therefore allows for more control over one's own business.

I was all excited for my first challenge, one hundred facials. I hit it pretty quickly. I started doing facials in some senior facilities. They were great and acted like recycled teenagers. They had great stories to tell and I loved listening to them and helping them feel pretty for a day.

After a few years, I was not as enthusiastic about finding new clients. I certainly don't turn down the opportunity to talk about Mary Kay products, when given the chance. I still had some regular clients and certainly did not turn anyone away. It is a great line of products, and the benefits are wonderful. Dwayne kept saying how young I looked. Of course, I told him that it was just good genes.

Cancer

In 2012, I went to the VA Hospital for my annual exam. I usually have a mammogram every other year. This year, they were insistent on me getting one. I finally agreed and scheduled the test. It was definitely a God thing. The first one came out suspicious, so they ordered a higher compression test and ultrasound. I went back in and had that one done. Dwayne said that this was sexist. He felt that men should do it too. I told him that he was absolutely right and I would love to see a man put his privates under such compression and see if they don't pass out. In reality, there are men who have had breast cancer, and from time to time, I do see a man getting a mammogram.

I was scheduled for a breast biopsy in January 2014. I am super sensitive to needles and told them to not show me any instruments. I had a tendency to pass out. Well, this was not an easy thing to do with my left breast in a vise and trying to look over my left shoulder to avoid looking at what the doctor had to do. They took a computer reading for placement of the six-inch long needle, then they made an incision for the needle. I passed out before the incision. They had to disconnect me from everything and lay me down on the bed with the air conditioner blowing on me. They must have had this happen fairly often if there was a bed in the room. We tried it again. Now, mind you, they have you in a chair that rolls up to the machine and locks down so you can't roll away. I made it through the imaging and the incision, but I briefly saw the needle, and I was out, again. They stopped and this time for good. When the doctor said that she may not have gotten enough, and that I would have to come back and do it again, I told them that dog don't hunt.

In the paperwork, I got before the procedure, it said that if I needed something to calm me down ahead of time to let them know. The front desk said that they would handle it in the back. The techs in the back said that they don't give you anything because that would require sedation, which would require a surgical tech and they don't do that there. Well then why did they put that information in the paperwork? The doctor said that would be a more invasive procedure, and I said, "And that would be different than this?"

The doctor called the next day and told me that what little she got looked suspicious and would schedule a lumpectomy and just go ahead and take it out.

I had the surgery on February 19, 2014. The doctor took out a jellied lump about the size of a large olive. She said that it would never have been found by self-examination. It was cancer, the lowest grade, but the highest category because it was about to breach the duct wall. I needed to start radiation, but would not need to lose my breast or undergo chemo. I fell apart for a few minutes. I called Dwayne crying to tell him the bad news.

I started praying long and hard. I had to hand this over to God or I would lose it completely. I told the kids; they were going to have to handle it with their spouses' support. I had enough on my plate at the moment. It took a day or two of praying, and I finally was able to give it to God. A comfort swept over me, and I knew that everything would be alright. Dwayne, on the other hand, had a problem dealing with it. I didn't know how to help him, except to pray for him.

At the time, I was taking two classes at HCC. One class, I had to drive in the morning to Katy, about thirty-five miles away, then out to the West Loop, about thirty miles from that to my evening class. Now I was about to start radiation. How was I going to make it to the VA Hospital in the Medical Center, which was further away, in between classes, and five days a week? What a pain in the neck. Dwayne insisted that I do the treatments closer. We had insurance and he didn't want me to be stressed out too much over this. I made arrangements for the MyFair Cancer Center to do the treatments under my insurance, but requested that they hold off billing until the end of the month, so the VA could get all their bills into the insurance and then all I would have to pay was the deductible. I tried to get the VA to pay for the radiation, but since they had the facilities to do this, they wanted me to come in there to take them. After many phone calls, I was finally able to get them to pay. In the meantime, the cancer center put in their bills early and got denied. Even after I told them to bill the VA, they continued to bill the insurance. I got really mad and told the insurance that they were double dipping, and they needed to request the money back from the facility. I told the cancer center to send the money back; they refused. The VA did eventually pay them. Whether or not they were able to get reimbursed from the insurance, I don't know. I still have to pay some of my co-pays.

The treatment took only about ten minutes. I was told to expect to get burns and maybe blisters, but they could provide me with some cream to help that. I decided to use my Mary Kay products since I was a consultant for Mary Kay. I figured that I needed to verify some of the products. I used them and did very well. By the fourth week, I was told that I would start blistering, but didn't. Some of the other women said they got some bad blisters, and it hurt terribly. I stuck to my products and didn't get burned except for a small area under my arm, where I hadn't gone up high enough with the lotion.

I did the treatments every day, five days a week, for six and a half weeks. This was done in between classes two days a week. It was a grueling schedule, but I managed to get it done and came out in pretty good shape. The doctor was impressed with the results of the products I was using. He even wrote a letter to Mary Kay for me on my behalf of his impressions. He was very pleased. I now recommend it to anyone going through radiation.

I finally graduated with an Associate's degree in Real Estate. I never thought that I'd earn a college degree. I was right, there was an exorbitant amount of reading to do. When I took the math classes, I felt really out of my element. I used to be pretty good in math. The instructor would ask me if I remembered how the formulas worked back in high school. I told her that was forty years ago, and no, I didn't.

Except for the Real Estate core classes, I was older than everyone in the classes, except for one class where the instructor was a bit older. She was my psych professor. She and I would joke about some of the old shows or attitudes from way back when.

I had to take an elective, so I got permission from the head of the department to let me take the Photography class. It was not on the list of approved classes. I had fun in it. I was able to get back into the darkroom and develop black and white film. A friend had given me her darkroom equipment, so I was able to set up a darkroom at home. I loved using the 35mm cameras. In the black and white medium, one can see more of the depth of field over the color films.

Climbing High

Dwayne and I have been together for thirty-three years. He is my rock. I love him more now than when we first got married. Everyone says that you have to work at marriage. Outside of the two times during the trials, we haven't had to work at anything, other than getting a job done. We communicate and respect each other. Without these, where would a relationship be? We enjoy target shooting, hiking, riding our motorcycles, and four-wheeling with our bad ass Ram Power Wagon. Ok, he really enjoys the four-wheeling. I have to admit that the trails in Colorado do have some really gnarly four-wheeling opportunities. I love doing things with and for Dwayne to make his life easier and giving ourselves more chances to be together. Sometimes a person just has to bite the bullet and do some things that really don't interest one's self, just to be together.

I am not afraid of doing hard work. When I set my mind to something, I do my best to finish it. I have been cancer free for three years now and pray for continued remission. I am self-sufficient and can shoot a gun, so what more can one ask of a spouse? We like a little competition with games and shooting, so things get a little heated when I beat him multiple times at either. All in fun, of course. Life is too short to sweat the small stuff, so we live and let live. We don't dictate what the other should or should not do. Dwayne isn't very romantic on a regular basis, but when he is, he usually nails it. We have fun living life at its fullest.

We still hike in the mountains in Wyoming and Colorado. We take our motorcycles and sometimes take our Power Wagon for some awesome four-wheeling. While in the mountains, we experience the most beautiful paintings God could have ever created. Even Dwayne acknowledges the fact that God created something really great. At night, the stars are bright as flashlights. Sometimes you can walk around with no light because the stars are so bright.

I usually have my camera and get some great pictures. I know that Dwayne thinks I'm crazy for some of the pictures I want to take. I will stop him frequently to get some shots off the side of the road, and he even makes the extra turn off when he sees something in the distance that would possibly be a great shot. One could take a thousand shots and get just a few worth the money. When we get home from a trip, I make a scrapbook of our travels and pick out the money shots. I have them enlarged, then I matte and frame them. I use recycled frames from thrift shops.

While on our trips, I find local beading or items that I can use in my jewelry making. One trip I found coyote claws and Indian-cut stones. That was a find. I enjoy making beautiful things out of God's creations. One trip, to Colorado, we were four-wheeling up Mount Princeton, over 14,000 feet. After arriving to the summit, there was a pile of boulders with a large cross sticking out of it. *(Cover Photo)* I was walking up to the top, where the cross was, while someone was coming down. He made a comment to me as he was passing, wondering if this was public land or private. I asked him what difference it made. He said that if it was public land, the cross shouldn't be there. How could anyone look out over the valley below and the mountains beyond and not see God in all of this? I told Dwayne this as we were walking down and around the crest to a cabin, which was built into the side of the mountain. This gentleman was coming back our way as we were heading in. On the side of the log cabin, in large letters, burned into the side of the cabin were the words, "Be still and know that I am God." Dwayne said, "I hope that ruined his vacation." We both laughed. How could anyone come up to the mountains and not believe that God made all that?

We've exposed our children to church, camping, bike riding, crafts, target shooting, and numerous other activities. We have taught them how to not be afraid to try new things and step out of their comfort zone. We plant the seeds, we hope that they grow into good, selfless, compassionate, moral, and loving adults. If a parent teaches their children how to fall, they should have no fear of getting up and should keep getting up, no matter how many say you can't.

When camping, we taught them to respect nature and all that God has given us. Camping in the wild can be dangerous, but uplifting. It builds character and teamwork. There is also no telling what will happen so one must expect the possibility of something going wrong or extremely right.

Sometimes one can walk into a forest and walk out into a different world than the one they came from. When we walk into the mountains, there are many parts of the trail that all we see is the side of a mountain and lots of trees, for a very long time, then, just around the next corner, it opens up into a beautiful valley below and mountains even higher in the background. Unfortunately, there are the switchbacks. These are the paths that wind back and forth, up or down a mountain, that will eventually get you hundreds of feet higher or lower in elevation. It is breathtaking. How can one say there is no God in the splendor of all this? Snowcapped peaks, green valleys and all the different colors and shades of the mountains are just some of the sites we enjoy.

Square Top Mountain (11,649 ft. in elevation) in Wyoming is one of our frequently visited mountains. We have tried to climb to the top of it three different times. First time, there was a fire in the area, another time, snow and ice kept us down, and we had trouble finding the path. Then the final try, we made it to about half way. It took us three hours to get to Granite Lake (9247 ft. in elevation) behind the mountain. We stopped for snacks and foot soaking at the lake and scoped out the other side that we still needed to navigate to get to the top. It looked as brutal as the first leg of the trip, except rockier. The first part was about a ninety-degree angle. We had to grab onto roots, limbs and vines to help ourselves climb up it. We just carried a day pack so we were not able to spend the night at the lake and head up to the top the following morning.

While soaking our feet we saw some fish swim by. We both just looked at each other and laughed; we had not brought our fishing poles. This would have been a great dinner treat, fresh trout. This would have been the thing to do. So, we headed back down after viewing the magnificent beauty of this place. On the way down, we used a walking stick to stop our feet from sliding down too far. It was pretty treacherous going down.

It is one of the most photographed mountains in Wyoming; most confuse it with Devil's Tower. Square Top Mountain is beautiful, as you can see, on the back cover. The time that it snowed and rained ice on us at Square Top, we decided to go to Aspen, Colorado, and climb West Maroon Pass, which is 12,500 feet in elevation. It had already snowed there and the weather was clearing. Greig was with us on this trip. We hiked in and made camp. The birds were really friendly. They would fly down onto our hands holding trail mix. Having water is usually not a problem in Wyoming. There is usually water in great supply, no matter where we camp. This time we had to hike a little bit further than usual, but there was water. We made camp off the main trail in the trees. The sky at night was always so beautiful. When night fell, we lay out on a rock or tarp and stargazed, looking for satellites. The following day we grabbed the day packs and headed up to the pass. We were at approximately 11,000 feet and still needed to get to 12,500. Greig kept saying that he would only go as far as the snow.

We stopped for a rest and some trail mix and watched a group of people coming down from the pass. Dwayne was starting to chicken out on going up. I reminded him of all his stories of previous trips with his friends, saying that they never wanted to go further and I had agreed to go with him. As the group got closer, we noticed that they were a bunch of senior citizens. We figured that a jeep tour dropped them off on the other side and then it would be downhill from there. They got within earshot of us and one told us that he was 83 and a retired general. That was all it took. Dwayne couldn't let an old man show him up.

We started up and got to the little patch of snow. There were tracks running through it. It looked like a rabbit and large cat. No doubt what was going on there.

Greig stopped there and went back to camp. Dwayne and I headed up to the pass. After about one hundred feet gained in elevation, the air started getting harder to breathe. Within thirty feet of the pass, a younger man was heading down. He told us that we were almost there. With every five steps, it took us five minutes to catch our breath. We finally made it up there and looked down the other side. We took back everything we had been thinking of those old folks. They had a steep trail to climb coming up the other side. It was beautiful up there as we looked down at valleys on both sides of the pass. I loved seeing the snowcapped mountains.

It is good to see now that our son, Jeremy, has taken his family to similar places and shows them the spirit of adventure. Sitting around a campfire, feeding the birds, squirrels, and raccoons, eating your trail mix, and four-wheeling. There is so much one can learn by communing with nature.

I take my camera with me when we hike, bike and four-wheel. I took hundreds of pictures and got a few pretty good ones. When looking through the lens, I sometimes regret that I just can't get the exact same thing that I am looking at with the naked eye. I regret that no matter how beautiful my pictures are, I can never get that excitement of looking at the bright stars at night or the moose and elk grazing just ten feet away.

Our dad always tried to live close and have a home available for any of us if we ever felt the need to come home. He tried to keep us together whenever possible, like Christmas. We've carried on and even added beach days in the summer time. We rent a house and let everyone know, so whoever can come is welcome, both family and adopted family (friends).

We have extended our family to close friends and some of them even look forward to our beach days and building sandcastles, games and fun in the sun.

Some people don't quite understand why we do this, especially having Christmas on another day, other than Christmas Day. For us, it is a renewal of our family commitment and the love we share with one another, as well as the need to keep our family together no matter where we are in our lives during the year. We know that Christmas and the beach times are coming. These are just a few times that we know for sure that our family will be together as we did when we were young.

As our families grow, and we all go our separate ways, we know that we are a family. No matter the miles or circumstances, we can count on each other to be there when called upon.

In 2005, there were five of us on a cruise to Mexico for Annette's 50th birthday. When we first arrived at customs, they went through everything. When they got to Annette's bag, the officer started laughing and called the others over to see the giant magnum of champagne that was in this small bag. Annette told them that her husband had gotten it for us all to celebrate her birthday. They thought it was cool. We had to take out the shelves in the tiny refrigerator to fit it in.

Brenda, Betsy, Annette, Gene and I all slept in one balcony room. It was tight, but also kind of fun. There was a storm brewing in the Caribbean and heading to the Gulf of Mexico, so they changed our destinations to Vera Cruz and Progresso. At one of the ports of call, we all piled into one taxi cab. We didn't want to take a chance of getting separated in a foreign country. We went to a beach, paid the taxi driver and asked him to return at a certain time. He didn't, so we had to find another cab at the beach to get us back to the ship. If you are not back by a certain time, the ship will sail without you; so, we wanted to get there on time.

At the other port of call, all but Gene got onto a bus and went to a rodeo. Gene went on a golf excursion. On the way, the leader was telling us how wonderful their avocadoes were. She went on and on about the avocadoes. We were served lunch and didn't see one avocado. The rodeo was different than we have in the U.S. They mostly showed us rope tricks and fancy horse maneuvers.

The highlight of our day was dinner. We all sat at one table to ourselves. The waiter was great. After the first night, he had our likes and dislikes down pretty good, even with Brenda being a vegetarian. The food was great. One day we participated in a little competition where they pulled Annette and a few others on stage to compete in games for prizes. Once we even competed in water games. It was all fun.

Hawaii

In 2006, eight of us went to Hawaii. Annette, Jacque, Ariana, Jeff, Marissa, Betsy, Dwayne and I all rented a house near the beach. Before we left Houston, the TSA agent was checking out Betsy's purse and found a bunch of lighters. Little did I know, this would be a precursor to future inspections. When we got to Hawaii, Jacque rented a van; Dwayne and I rented a car for us. We wanted to explore the island of Oahu.

I had read a trail book about some of the trails that would be good one-day hikes. On the way to the house from the airport, Dwayne was in a bad mood. He wasn't all that excited about flying so far. He didn't see anything that impressed him any better than Wyoming. When we got to the house, I told Betsy that we needed to get him out on a hike as soon as possible. The following day Dwayne, Betsy, Annette and I went on a hike. It was a really green and lush forest with beautiful flowers sprinkled around. We came to a swimming hole with a waterfall. While Betsy was changing into her swimsuit, she put her glasses on a tree and forgot them there. When we returned to the house, we were all pulling out our spare glasses for her to try out. She managed to get by until a few days later when she and Dwayne hiked back to get hers. When we left, mine were left behind at the house. I had to have the owner mail them to me.

Dwayne and I went on an excursion on little four-wheelers through the valley in which several films were done, like Jurassic Park and Pearl Harbor. Dwayne, Betsy, and I toured around the island in a glider where Betsy and I were in one plane and Dwayne was in another. Our pilot had been in Guam in the Air Force, so we chatted enough that we actually got a few extra minutes in the air. He showed us where the communication station was that thought the Japanese planes were U.S. planes coming in from California.

Everywhere we went, we learned more about what actually happened during the Pearl Harbor attack.

We all went to the Cultural Center where we had an authentic luau with dancers. The college students put on a great show.

We were so glad that we had seen the island before the Pearl Harbor Museum. We had to watch a thirty-minute film, then they took us out to the Arizona Memorial. I don't think there was a dry eye in the room after the film. The experience was sobering. After seeing the different parts of the island, this information we received at the museum made more sense. We knew where they were talking about, when they talked about where the planes came in, and what mountain range they were talking about.

When we got ready to leave the island, the customs agent found a few pocket knives in Betsy's purse. We couldn't believe that the Houston agents didn't find them.

About six weeks later, Betsy, Dwayne, and I flew to Wyoming. Greig met us there. When leaving there, she was stopped with plastic bottles too large for acceptance. I decided that maybe I didn't want to fly with her anymore.

We had a great time together hiking up to the Bomber Falls area. One day a young moose came through the campsite. We all stayed real still until he passed on. They can be aggressive, if provoked.

The altitude got to Dwayne and me, maybe because we flew in. Usually we drove up and took little hikes on the way to Wyoming. That helped to get us acclimated. I really don't want to fly in and hike again. Getting into the higher elevations, it gets tough.

It was fun having my sister with us for once. She and Greig had been dating, so it was nice having the four of us together doing something we all enjoyed.

In 2009, Dwayne and Greig turned fifty so we decided to get together in Tampa, where Greig lived. Dwayne, Betsy and I, flew into Tampa. Dwayne's parents, Faith and Larry, drove out too. Betsy had been flying out to Tampa on four separate occasions trying to catch a nighttime lift off of the shuttle. We all decided to drive to the East coast to catch the nighttime shuttle lift off. They had postponed it several times and maybe it was going to actually happen this time. We staked out our spot in a park and waited for hours to see it. It finally took off. This was my second time to see a nighttime lift off. I was on the west coast of Florida last time and this was pretty cool to see it closer. One can only get about ten miles away to see it, so we had about the best seats possible. All those videos we see on the news are from cameras up close and some with telephoto lenses that the professionals use.

Betsy was messing with us since she had been coming so many times to see it and never did. We came out and it happened with our first time.

In 2010, it was my turn to be fifty. My sisters asked me what I wanted to do for my birthday. I told them that I wanted to go deep sea fishing. We took a trip out of Freeport on a boat with about eighty or so onboard. Dwayne, Betsy, Annette, Gene, a couple of neighbors, and I went. When we arrived at five in the morning, there was a man still drunk from the night before. His buddies had backed out of the trip. I helped him get his cooler onboard. The rest of the trip, he was hitting on me. Around lunch time, we were under the covered area eating when this man fell asleep on the floor, totally passed out. He was shirtless, so I put a couple of donuts with cherries in the middle on his chest. Dwayne thought that was mean, but I told him that this guy had been hitting on me all day. He conceded that I was in the right and he deserved it.

While fishing, Dwayne had paid one of the deck hands fifty dollars to take care of us. There was a blond-haired young woman at the front of the boat that soon took off her shirt and there went the deck hand. He then paid another hand fifty dollars to take care of us. Dwayne didn't tell us this until later at the house. Gene had wondered why us girls were getting so much attention.

Dwayne told him that the blonde cost him fifty dollars; Gene just laughed. I had caught the first, the largest and the most fish from our group. We all had a great time.

This year, 2017, Dwayne had the worst March in his life, health-wise. He got shingles one day, then two days later, he got his top teeth taken out and implants put in. The following week, he threw out his back, then the week following that, he cracked a rib. In May, I had knee surgery. He was a great helper, in spite of his ailments. The shingles cleared up, but the ribs and teeth were still bothering him. I learned to finally shut up and let him help me. I was able to hobble along with my crutches, but it hurt pretty badly for a couple of weeks.

I have many photographs; many in albums and many in scrapbooks. Once in a while, we pull them out to reminisce about when they were taken. Sometimes, we think that we haven't done much with our lives, but when we look at the photographs of the mountains, waterfalls, children, family, and friends, we see that our lives have been filled with much love and happenings. I tell Dwayne, that when we get older and can't remember events, we'll have plenty of pictures to refresh our memories.

Before Gavin was born, I started working on scrapbooks for him. One was of his grandpa, aunt, daddy, and I. Then, I started one of his adventures from when he was still inside his mama's womb at the baby shower. Over the years, we have filled it with many events and adventures that he will not remember, but will see that we lived a full life with him as our focus. God blessed us with a few years that we were able to do a lot of things with him and his dad.

I have made all sorts of scrapbooks with just my side of the family, from when we got together for our beach days and Christmas. It is fun to see other's reactions when they see them. It creates a lot of laughing and reminiscing. Our family has come a long way from those days of separation and turmoil. We all have our own families and adventures.

Dwayne and I have created many adventures ourselves, with our children. When I look back at all that I have gone through, I thank God for all the blessings that he has bestowed upon my life. There were many times that I wanted to give up, but Jesus kept nudging me forward. By looking at our lives through pictures, I know that I could not have chosen a better husband and father in Dwayne. I could not have done any of this without God in my life. Jesus had definitely blessed our lives.

Nowadays, I play cards with a group of friends at the Hockley Community Center. We play "Pennies from Heaven". It is a canasta game. There are six to eight of us that keep a game going for a few hours every Friday. At our Friday lunch and game time, we are probably the loudest table in the place. There are about five or six tables playing 42, two tables playing Mexican Train and two tables playing Pennies. We have been told that we have too much fun at our table. We talk about everything from our grandkids to what is going on in the neighborhoods around us, and we laugh a lot. We even break into a song from time to time. I am probably the youngest one there and I'm fifty-seven. I call us all a bunch of old recycled teenagers. It gets pretty crazy with our group, but I couldn't ask for better friends.

We take turns hosting a Wednesday lunch and card day, so we get to try out each other's cooking. Anne has started to join us on our Wednesdays. This started when she showed up at the center with flowers for my birthday and stayed to play with us. She fit into our little group just fine. This is one more thing that I am so grateful for, that I have a good relationship with my daughter, one that I never had with my mother.

My canasta friends have become part of my extended family now. I love that we can call upon each other for encouragement and assistance when needed.

What some may call friends, with us, we call our extended family. These are a special group of people that we feel that we can share our innermost thoughts, without judgement, and know that they would be there for us if we really needed them to be and they know that we would be there for them. This stems back to the saying, "It takes a village to raise a family." Well, I believe that it takes a community to live a life worth living.

Thank you, my family and friends for your wonderful support and encouragement.

Mae Edwards
Email:
mae@stolenoptions.com